Overcoming Trauma

Companion Workbook

Allison Smiley

Overcoming Trauma

Companion Workbook

AllisonSmiley.com

Author photograph by Austin DuBois

ISBN 978-1-08797-996-0 (paperback)
ISBN 978-1-08797-998-4 (ebook)

Printed in the United States.

Although the author has made every effort to ensure that the information in this book was correct at press time, the author does not assume and hereby disclaims any liability to any party for any loss, damage, or disruption caused by errors or omissions, whether such errors or omissions result from negligence, accident, or any other cause.

This workbook is not intended as a substitute for the medical advice of physicians. The reader should regularly consult a physician in matters relating to his/her health and particularly with respect to any symptoms that may require diagnosis or medical attention.

OVERCOMING TRAUMA

Workbook Contents

Welcome 1

Module 1

Lesson 1.1	ACEs & The Four F's	4
Lesson 1.2	Breathwork	8
Lesson 1.3	Orienting	9
Lesson 1.4	Meditative Yoga	10
Lesson 1.5	Mindfulness	11
Lesson 1.6	Meditation	13

Module 2

Lesson 2.1	Map of Consciousness	18
Lesson 2.2	Law of Attraction	20
Lesson 2.3	Positive Thought Momentum	23
Lesson 2.4	Destination Vibration	24
Lesson 2.5	Violet Flame	25
Lesson 2.6	Balancing Chakras	30

Module 3

Lesson 3.1	Levels of Consciousness	42
Lesson 3.2	Resistance vs Allowing	43
Lesson 3.3	Mantras	47
Lesson 3.4	Observing & Rescripting	48
Lesson 3.5	Gratitude	50
Lesson 3.6	Guided Meditation	54

Module 4

Lesson 4.1	Spiritual Bypassing	58
Lesson 4.2	Feel and Heal Process	59
Lesson 4.3	Journal Time	63
Lesson 4.4	Positive Affirmations	65
Lesson 4.5	Self-Compassion	68
Lesson 4.6	Radical Acceptance	69

Module 5

Lesson 5.1	Live from the Heart	76
Lesson 5.2	Heart Math	80
Lesson 5.3	Ask the Heart	84
Lesson 5.4	Heart Mantras	86
Lesson 5.5	Journey into the Heart	87
Lesson 5.6	Gratitude and Appreciation	88

Module 6

Lesson 6.1	What is Forgiveness	94
Lesson 6.2	Ho'oponopono	97
Lesson 6.3	Forgiveness Prayers	99
Lesson 6.4	Forgiveness Affirmations	101
Lesson 6.5	Forgiveness Meditation	105
Lesson 6.6	Forgiveness Worksheets	106
Lesson 6.7	Self-Forgiveness Worksheet	109

Module 7

Lesson 7.1	Self-Love vs Self-Care	114
Lesson 7.2	Extreme Self-Care	117
Lesson 7.3	Self-Care for the Body	118
Lesson 7.4	Self-Care for the Mind	126
Lesson 7.5	Self-Care for the Spirit	129
Lesson 7.6	Self-Care for the Emotions	133

Module 8

Lesson 8.1	The Power of Persistance	140
Lesson 8.2	A Quick Lookback	143
Lesson 8.3	Make a Plan	148
Lesson 8.4	Create a Daily Routine	150
Lesson 8.5	Putting it All Together	153
Lesson 8.6	Celebrate YOU	156

References	158
About the Author	161

Take time
to do the
things that
make your
SOUL
happy.

A Letter From Allison

Hello my beautiful friend,

A HUGE welcome to you. I'm so delighted that you made the decision to pick up this copy of the *Overcoming Trauma Companion Workbook*.

This is going to be a pretty incredible journey and I'm **delighted and honored** to be on this path with you. So many people have experienced beautiful transformations from the 8-step healing program that I've outlined in my book, and I hope you will too.

When I first started on my healing journey, I had no clue where to even begin. It was a very confusing, frustrating, and overwhelming time for me. I was figuring it out by trial and error (often trial by fire!) and it was pretty disheartening to say the least.

I've made it my mission to provide the tools, support, and empowerment you've been searching for. I designed this program specifically with *YOU* in mind...to remove the guesswork and guide you through the process.

There are additional free supplemental materials for the book and workbook available for you. For access, just go to overcomingtrauma.allisonsmiley.com and register. I will continue to add more videos, audios, and worksheets as I create them, so keep checking in the portal for new items that have been uploaded.

Finally, if you would like additional support, I offer private coaching sessions to personally guide you through the steps and help you deepen your healing process. For more information go to allisonsmiley.com/alignment-coaching.

Love and Blessings,

Allison

CONNECT WITH ME

MODULE 1

BUILDING
RESILIENCE

The Four F's

Types of Trauma Response

Descriptions of the four types of trauma responses. Many people are often a hybrid of these, but we usually have one that is our go-to trauma response.

FIGHT:

An aggressive response that is triggered by a perceived threat. And it can manifest in ways such as bullying, picking fights verbally or physically, raging, aggressive driving, or degrading others.

This type has a belief that power and control can create a feeling of safety, secure love and prevent painful feelings of abandonment.

Think of this response as being similar to a lion with a thorn in its paw. He can be mean and dangerous if he feels threatened, but underneath he's really just hurting and needs some nurturing.

FLIGHT:

A fleeing response such as walking out of a perceived threatening situation, moving, breaking up a relationship or friendship, or changing jobs.

It can also be demonstrated in not just a physical fleeing but fleeing by going into overdrive or a hyperactive state and can manifest as going nonstop, focusing only on getting things done, to-do lists, running errands, never-ending projects, and can often take place in a frantic way with lack of direction.

This type has an unconscious belief that perfection will make them safe and loveable. They are also susceptible to stimulant addiction and addiction to their own adrenaline as well as process addictions such as busyness.

FREEZE:

This response is like a numbing out, checking out mentally, realizing that resisting is futile and could potentially cause harm.

This trauma response would be demonstrated in Netflix binges, computer gaming, and laying down or sleeping a lot.

There is a belief here that safety is found in solitude. Where the flight type is stuck in the 'on' position, the freeze type can be perceived as stuck in the 'off' position.

Freeze types often dissociate, daydream and disconnect. They are prone to opioid or sedating substance addictions and avoid social situations due to the fear of feeling abandonment pain.

FAWN:

A response that consists of trying to please others or finding ways to be helpful in order to avoid harm or attack.

This trauma response type typically takes on the needs and wants of others and doesn't have a clear idea of their own, having given them up early in life to keep peace or avoid attack.

There is a belief that they have to give up their own needs, rights, and boundaries in order to experience love and safety.

They are usually the child of a narcissistic parent and were often shamed or scared out of developing a healthy sense of ego.

What is my trauma response type?

Adverse Childhood Experiences (ACEs)

1   Did a parent or other adult in the household often or very often... Swear at you, insult you, put you down, or humiliate you? or Act in a way that made you afraid that you might be physically hurt?

No___   If Yes, enter 1 ___

2   Did a parent or other adult in the household often or very often... Push, grab, slap, or throw something at you? or Ever hit you so hard that you had marks or were injured?

No___   If Yes, enter 1 ___

3   Did an adult or person at least 5 years older than you ever... Touch or fondle you or have you touch their body in a sexual way? or Attempt or actually have oral, anal, or vaginal intercourse with you?

No___   If Yes, enter 1 ___

4   Did you often or very often feel that ... No one in your family loved you or thought you were important or special? or Your family didn't look out for each other, feel close to each other, or support each other?

No___   If Yes, enter 1 ___

5   Did you often or very often feel that ... You didn't have enough to eat, had to wear dirty clothes, and had no one to protect you? or Your parents were too drunk or high to take care of you or take you to the doctor if you needed it?

No___   If Yes, enter 1 ___

6   Were your parents ever separated or divorced?

No___   If Yes, enter 1 ___

7   Was your mother or stepmother:
Often or very often pushed, grabbed, slapped, or had something thrown at her? or Sometimes, often, or very often kicked, bitten, hit with a fist, or hit with something hard? or Ever repeatedly hit over at least a few minutes or threatened with a gun or knife?

No___   If Yes, enter 1 ___

8   Did you live with anyone who was a problem drinker or alcoholic, or who used street drugs?

No___   If Yes, enter 1 ___

9   Was a household member depressed or mentally ill, or did a household member attempt suicide?

No___   If Yes, enter 1 ___

10   Did a household member go to prison?

No___   If Yes, enter 1 ___

Now add up your "Yes" answers: _____   This is your ACEs Score.

Lesson 1.2

People who have experienced trauma or are under chronic, high levels of stress tend to have very short, shallow breathing. I don't know why it's called breathwork because it is one of the quickest and easiest ways to calm your nerves, energize, and center yourself.

Pranayama is a yogic term for control over the energy in the breath. It provides quick and efficient ways to tap into the nervous system. Research has shown how breathwork relieves stress and anxiety and helps with trauma recovery.

Calming Breath

Use this before bed, at work, or anytime you need to get grounded, centered, and calm your nervous system.

Alternate Nostril Breathing

This type of breathing calms, balances, and unites the right and left sides of the brain. It's great for releasing fatigue, headaches, and tension.

Dragon Breath

This is an energizing breathing technique and great when you wake up in the morning. Some people say this breathwork has a similar effect on their energy as drinking a cup of coffee.

Watch the videos on how to do these breathing practices in the free Supplemental Materials portal at overcomingtrauma.allisonsmiley.com.

Lesson 1.3

Orienting

People with trauma are typically on constant high alert and everything can feel threatening. The process of moving the head and the neck to scan around you, allows the limbic brain and nerves on the back of the neck to realize that all is well and it's OK to relax.

Orienting with Senses

This mindfulness exercise allows you to bring your awareness to your body and the present moment through the senses. It is a great one to use when you're feeling triggered or if you frequently dissociate.

Watch the videos on how to do these orienting practices in the free Supplemental Materials portal at overcomingtrauma.allisonsmiley.com.

Lesson 1.4

Meditative Flow Yoga

There has been increasing awareness regarding how yoga can aid in healing trauma. Bessel Van der Kolk, a leading trauma researcher, recommends incorporating mindful or meditative yoga into trauma treatment. There are several reasons for this.

First, traumatized people often get stuck in powerlessness because they were unable to or were prevented from taking action at the time of the trauma, such as fighting or fleeing, and their body needs to complete the action.

Second, dissociation is a common symptom of trauma and creates a disconnect from the body. People with trauma need to reconnect with the sensations in the body and release trapped energies and emotions connected to the trauma.

Finally, trauma survivors' bodies get taken over when triggered by loud sounds, criticism, or hurtful things, and they need to engage the body in a mindful way in order to release stress hormones and reset the critical areas of the brain. Mindful or meditative yoga is a way to calm the mind and feel safe and present in the body.

Watch the videos on how to do meditative flow yoga practices in the free Supplemental Materials portal at overcomingtrauma.allisonsmiley.com.

Lesson 1.5

Mindfulness Practices

Using mindfulness can be a great way to get centered and present in your body and in the moment. Here are a few ways to incorporate mindfulness into your day.

Daily activities:

You can use mindfulness during daily activities such as washing the dishes or brushing your teeth. Pay attention to the water flowing onto the dishes or the feel of the toothbrush in your hand. By becoming aware of yourself or of sensations as you're doing an activity, you bring your attention to the present moment.

Incorporate the Senses:

This is another way to use mindfulness in your day. As you are walking feel your feet on the ground, or notice the sounds or smells around you, pay attention to the taste and texture of your food as you eat it. By incorporating the senses into your activities, it brings your awareness into the present moment and into your body.

Do a Body Scan:

Sit in a comfortable position in a chair. Bring your awareness to your breath and notice each breath as you inhale and exhale. Begin to notice the bottoms of your feet and become aware of any sensations in your feet. Gradually take your awareness up your body until you reach the top of your head and notice the sensations or feelings in your body as you go.

Observe an Object for 5 Minutes:

Use mindfulness by taking 5 minutes to observe an object, its features such as color, texture, sound (if any), the purpose of the object, etc.

What mindfulness practices did I use this week?

1

What was my experience with the mindfulness practices?

2

What I noticed while I was doing these mindfulness practices:

3

What I found helpful by incorporating mindfulness into my day:

4

Lesson 1.6

Meditation Practices

Incorporating meditation into your daily routine can be a great way to heal your body and release stuck energy and trauma. Even just 10-15 minutes a day can make a huge difference!

Count Your Breaths:

The breath is the focus of this meditation. Try to focus on the rhythm of your breathing. To make your focus easier, you'll count every breath in and every breath out.

Every time your mind wanders, simply return your focus to your breathing and begin counting again. Notice the sensations of your breath as you inhale and exhale. You can breathe in and out through your nose or in through your nose and out through your mouth, whatever is more comfortable for you.

Do this for 5-10 minutes daily and increase the time at whatever pace feels comfortable to you.

Mantra:

With this meditation, a sound, a word, a sentence or an affirmation is the focus of your meditation. Similar to counting breaths, you'll focus your attention on the word or words of your mantra.

In a relaxed seated position, begin to focus on your mantra. You can repeat the words quietly in your mind or out loud, whichever you prefer. You can sync the words to your breaths if you wish.

For example, if your mantra is "Letting go" you can breathe in to "Letting" and breathe out to "go". Do this for 5-10 minute daily and increase the time at whatever pace feels comfortable to you.

What meditation practices did I use this week?

What was my experience with the meditation practices?

What I noticed while I was doing these meditation practices:

What I found helpful by incorporating meditation into my day:

"The more you praise and celebrate your life, the more there is in life to celebrate."

– Oprah Winfrey

MODULE 2

RAISING YOUR VIBRATION

Lesson 2.1

Map of Consciousness

The scale of consciousness rates different levels of awareness, the emotions, and the life-views associated with them. You can consciously work your way up the scale to shift your vibration higher.

God-View	Life-View	Level	Log	Emotion	Process	
Self	Is	ENLIGHTENMENT	700-1000	Ineffable	Pure	P O W E R
All-Being	Perfect	PEACE	600	Bliss	Illumination	
One	Complete	JOY	540	Serenity	Transfiguration	
Loving	Benign	LOVE	500	Reverence	Revelation	
Wise	Meaningful	REASON	400	Understanding	Abstraction	
Merciful	Harmonious	ACCEPTANCE	350	Forgiveness	Transcendence	
Inspiring	Hopeful	WILLINGNESS	310	Optimism	Intention	
Enabling	Satisfactory	NEUTRALITY	250	Trust	Release	
Permitting	Feasible	COURAGE	200	Affirmation	Empowerment	
Indifferent	Demanding	PRIDE	175	Scorn	Inflation	F O R C E
Vengeful	Antagonistic	ANGER	150	Hate	Aggression	
Denying	Disappointing	DESIRE	125	Craving	Enslavement	
Punitive	Frightening	FEAR	75	Anxiety	Withdrawal	
Disdainful	Tragic	GRIEF	75	Regret	Despondency	
Condemning	Hopeless	APATHY	50	Despair	Abdication	
Vindictive	Evil	GUILT	30	Blame	Destruction	
Despise	Miserable	SHAME	20	Humiliation	Elimination	

Where am I at on the map of consciousness? Do I go up and down by default and knee jerk reactions?

What are some ways that I can consciously move up the scale and raise my vibration?

How can I incorporate these activities into my day?

Who are my support people that can help me with these goals?

Lesson 2.2

1. It is POSSIBLE to experience what you want in life
2. You DESERVE (Worthy of) what you want
3. You can TRUST that the Universe has your back
4. The Universe is ABUNDANT and wants to deliver your desires
5. Attraction is EASY
6. You are RESPONSIBLE for everything you attract
7. You have the POWER to attract whatever you align your vibration to

1. Is it POSSIBLE to experience what you want in life?

2. Do you believe that you DESERVE what you want?

3. Do you TRUST that the Universe has your back or do you doubt?

4. Do you believe in ABUNDANCE?

5. Is attraction EASY and EFFORTLESS?

6. Does it feel good to feel RESPONSIBLE for everything you attract?

7. Do you feel you have the POWER to attract your desires?

1. It is POSSIBLE to experience what you want in life
2. You DESERVE (Worthy of) what you want
3. You can TRUST that the Universe has your back
4. The Universe is ABUNDANT and wants to deliver your desires
5. Attraction is EASY
6. You are RESPONSIBLE for everything you attract
7. You have the POWER to attract whatever you align your vibration to

FEAR-BASED CORE BELIEF SYSTEMS

1. Defectiveness (Unworthy, Bad, Wrong, Imperfect)
2. Alone (Unlovable, Abandoned)
3. Helpless / Unsafe (Powerless, Victim, Suffering)
4. Entitlement (Justification, No Effort)
5. Responsibility (Caretaking, Self-Sacrifice)
6. Scarcity (Not Enough, Impossibility)

THOUGHT HABITS

1. Mind-Reading (Projecting about others thoughts/feelings)
2. Filtering (Negative Mind focus)
3. Polarized Thinking (Everything is Awful or Great; ALL or NOTHING)
4. Overgeneralization (Sweeping thoughts based on scanty evidence)
5. Catastrophizing (Assuming the worst case scenario)
6. Magnifying (Enlarge the bad, minimize the good)
7. Personalization (Comparing, Assuming others' events are about you)
8. Shoulds (Expectation, Judgements, Arbitrary rules for behavior)
9. Non-sequiturs (Linking irrational thoughts based on false premises)

What are my Fear-Based Core Beliefs and Thought Habits?

Setting Intentions

Think about what you want to create in your life. Sometimes it's easier to identify what you DON'T want and then shift it into what you DO want.

Ex: Too sick to do things that I enjoy   Strong, healthy, able to jog and play tennis

What I Don't Want:	What I Do Want:

Lesson 2.3

Develop 4 Thoughts to Create a

Positive Thought Momentum

4 Thoughts x 17 Seconds = Positive Vibration Momentum. Practice this Vibration Daily.

Thought #1

Thought #2

Thought #3

Thought #4

Lesson 2.4

Destination Vibration

It's now time to create a destination vibration. The destination vibration builds upon the Positive Thought Momentum and Law of Attraction principles you have already been practicing.

The destination vibration takes your list of goals and intentions and brings it to life in your mind and body and incorporates the senses and emotions, so that you're feeling, seeing, experiencing your life as if your intentions have already manifested. It's very powerful!

Grab your list of goals and intentions and then listen to the audio recording in the free Supplemental Materials to create your destination vibration.

From Kim Beekman's Inner Alignment Program

24

Lesson 2.5

The Violet Flame

The Violet Flame is an easy, quick, and efficient tool to use and you can do it from anywhere. It is made up of love (pink), wisdom (gold), and power (blue), and when these are combined, they create the violet flame.

Violet is the highest vibrating color of transmutation, fire is the fastest form of transformation, and together they become an amazing way to transmute, transform, and transcend lower vibrating energies, thoughts, patterns, and beliefs.

Listen to the Violet Flame meditation in the Supplemental Materials.

Violet Flame Invocations

Here are a few ways to use the Violet Flame to transmute, transform, and transcend lower vibrating energies, thoughts, patterns, and beliefs. Try them out and see what ones work best for you. You can do these any time and anywhere!

Before using the invocations below, first visualize a column of divine white light surrounding you for protection. Flowing infinitely up and infinitely down, flowing through you and all around you.

Invocation #1

I invoke the Violet Flame to flow in, through, up, and around my physical body, my etheric body, my emotional body, and my mental body. Transmuting any and all lower vibrating energies into the highest vibration possible, filling my physical body and luminous energy field with the highest vibration of love and light that I can comfortably handle now. (Visualize your body and energy field being filled with violet light).

Invocation #2

- *I call upon the Violet Flame to surround me now, to clear my energy and raise my vibration.*
- *I call upon the Violet Flame to surround me now, to clear my energy and raise my vibration.*
- *I call upon the Violet Flame to surround me now, to clear my energy and raise my vibration.*
- *(Visualize your body and energy field being filled with violet light).*

Invocation #3

I AM the Violet Consuming Flame in action.

I AM the Violet Consuming Flame in action.

I AM the Violet Consuming Flame in action.

Invocation #4 (Longer version)

Mighty I AM Presence, Beloved God, My Heavenly Source, Please make manifest in me now the Sacred Violet Flame of Transmutation. Bring the Violet Flame into every cell, molecule and atom of my body filling me totally and completely.

Blessed Violet Flame blaze into my Heart and expand out and around all of my bodies, physical, emotional, mental and spiritual, surrounding my entire Being with your Divine Grace, Love, Mercy and Forgiveness.

Transmute all karma, negative thoughts, actions, deeds and energy that I have ever created at any time, in all dimensions, on all levels, in all bodies, through all time and space, past, present and future, for all Eternity.

Transmute everything that no longer serves me in body, mind and spirit; including false beliefs, lower emotions, and physical challenges.
Violet Flame transmute this current issue I wish to change in my life (describe issue). . . . turn it into (state desired result).

Transmute anything and everything that stands in my way of embodying the Ascended Christ Being of That I AM.

Beloved Violet Flame turn all that has been transmuted Into the Gold and Platinum Light of God, the Christ Consciousness, The Light of God that never fails.

Send this Gold and Platinum Light to me now, filling and surrounding my entire body with its Divine Radiance. Raise my vibration and frequency to the highest level possible for me at this time.

So Be It and So It Is. Thank You God. Amen.

From *The Spirit Mountain Chronicle*, 2007.

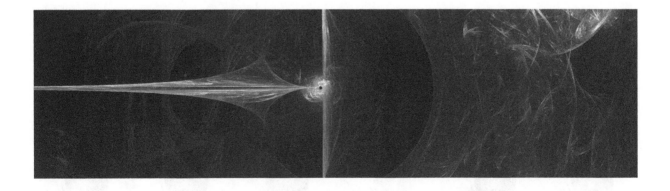

This is a fun way to incorporate the Violet Flame into your daily practice routine. Track your progress with the chart below.

Other ideas for using the Violet Flame:

① Clear karma and past life issues

② Use it on your home, car, workplace, neighborhood, city, planet

③ Breathe it into your heart to clear fear, anxiety, and worry

④ Clear communication lines, misunderstandings, cash flow blocks

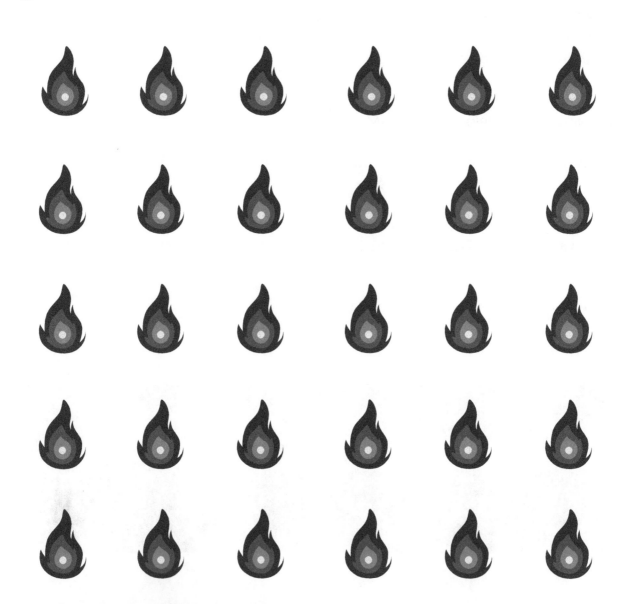

_____
_____
_____
_____
_____
_____
_____
_____
_____
_____
_____
_____
_____
_____
_____
_____
_____
_____
_____
_____
_____
_____
_____
_____
_____
_____
_____
_____
_____

Lesson 2.6

The 7 Chakras

Chakras are the energy centers in the body that are responsible for the flow of life energy, also known as chi or prana.

There are seven main chakras that are located along different points on the body, and they are connected to various organs and glands within the body.

Each of the chakras carries a specific meaning, is associated with a color, and influences different areas of our life and health.

Stress, lifestyle, negative thoughts, habits, or patterns can create a disturbance or block in the energy flow of chakras. When a chakra is disrupted or blocked, the life energy also gets blocked, and it creates issues in our lives on all levels – physical, emotional, mental, and spiritual.

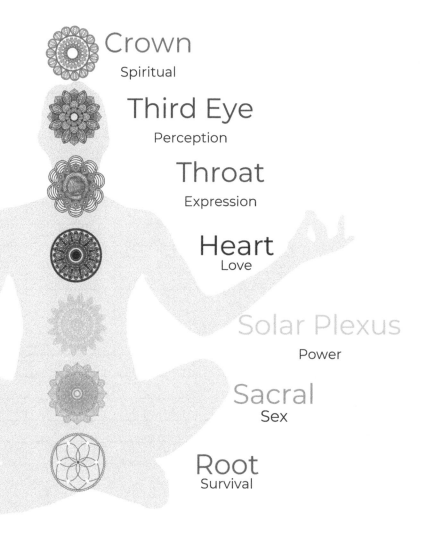

Crown
Spiritual

Third Eye
Perception

Throat
Expression

Heart
Love

Solar Plexus
Power

Sacral
Sex

Root
Survival

Spiritual Connection & Wisdom — 7 — Crown: Connection with Source, Wisdom, Universal Consciousness

3rd Eye: Clarity, Vision, Christ, Consciousness — 6 — Intuition & Beauty

Communication & TRUTH — 5 — Throat: Expression, Imagination, Life Purpose, Speak & Be Heard

Heart: Give/Receive LOVE Self-Esteem, Self-Love, ANXIETY — 4 — Love & Self-Esteem

Willpower & Peace — Solar Plexus: Will Power, Action, Motivation, Transformation, Self-Worth, ANGER

Sacral: Feeling, Intimacy, Desire, Socializing, Manifestation, GUILT — 2 — Sexuality and Harmony

Safety & Trust — 1 — Root: Survival, Grounding, Financial, Belonging, FEAR

Sit quietly in meditation or relaxed state and focus on each of the 7 chakras. Scan your body and do an inventory on how that part of the body feels. Become aware (observing without judgment) of imbalances related to the different layers of the body – physical, mental, emotional, spiritual.

For example, my Heart chakra:

Physically – My chest is tight and restricted

Emotionally – I am feeling anxious, overwhelmed

Mentally – I have looping thoughts, repeating negative thought patterns and beliefs ie: not good enough

Spiritually – not trusting in the divine, energy feels disconnected from Source love

1 Root Chakra:

Physically: _____
_____

Emotionally: _____
_____

Mentally: _____
_____

Spiritually: _____
_____

2 Sacral Chakra:

Physically: _____
_____

Emotionally: _____
_____

Mentally: _____
_____

Spiritually: _____
_____

3 Solar Plexus Chakra:

Physically: _____
_____

Emotionally: _____
_____

Mentally: _____
_____

Spiritually: _____
_____

4 Heart Chakra:

Physically: _____

_____

Emotionally: _____

_____

Mentally: _____

_____

Spiritually: _____

_____

5 Throat Chakra:

Physically: _____

_____

Emotionally: _____

_____

Mentally: _____

_____

Spiritually: _____

_____

6 Third Eye Chakra:

Physically: _____
_____

Emotionally: _____
_____

Mentally: _____
_____

Spiritually: _____
_____

7 Crown Chakra:

Physically: _____
_____

Emotionally: _____
_____

Mentally: _____
_____

Spiritually: _____
_____

My Main Imbalances Are:

_____
_____
_____
_____
_____
_____
_____
_____
_____
_____
_____
_____
_____
_____
_____
_____
_____
_____
_____
_____
_____
_____
_____
_____
_____
_____
_____
_____
_____
_____
_____
_____
_____

We all carry some type of unworthiness beliefs that are stored in the vibrational makeup of our bodies and energy fields. When we experience trauma, these beliefs get anchored in deep into the fabric of our being.

> Neglected = Unlovable
>
> Abandoned = Unvaluable
>
> Punished = Bad
>
> Criticized = Failure

We create these belief systems based upon factors from our childhood. None of it is actually true, even if it feels like it is. We are able to rewire the **truth** of unconditional worthiness into these false belief systems.

Example belief: *"I am unlovable and a failure"*

Criticized, judged, expected to be perfect

Rewarded for beauty, achievements, and successes

Identity was based upon results and looks

Triggered in relationships when I wasn't validated, acknowledged, or tone implied my failure or shortcomings

Part of our trauma healing work is to shift and rewire these beliefs and realize that we are inherently worthy **no matter what**. We were taught to search for this outside of ourselves, but we are fully lovable, worthy, and good **right now and always!**

How Does Your Trauma Anchor You?

_____
_____
_____
_____
_____
_____
_____
_____
_____
_____
_____
_____
_____

My Core Beliefs or Unworthiness Types Are:

_____
_____
_____
_____
_____
_____
_____
_____
_____
_____
_____
_____
_____
_____
_____
_____
_____

We have seven energetic layers that make up our energy field. Every living thing is made up of a vibrational frequency that radiates beyond our physical bodies. It is commonly referred to as the aura, subtle body, or energy field.

Each energetic layer connects to the physical body through a chakra. Sensing blocks in the energy field can help us identify issues before they become a physical problem in the body.

Though our trauma healing work and daily practices, we release the blocks, dense vibration, and beliefs that have been anchored in the energy field.

Chakra		Body
Crown Chakra Spirituality		Causal Body Mental Aspect
Third Eye Chakra Awareness		Celestial Body Emotional Aspect
Throat Chakra Communication		Etheric Template Higher Physical Aspect
Heart Chakra Love Healing		Astral Body
Solar Plexus Chakra Wisdom Power		Mental Body Lower Mental Aspect
Sacral Chakra Sexuality Creativity		Emotional Body Lower Emotional Aspect
Root Chakra Basic Trust	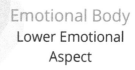	Etheric Body Lower Aspect

Your mind will always
believe what you tell it.

Feed it hope.
Feed it truth.
Feed it love.

MODULE 3
MANAGING YOUR THOUGHTS

Lesson 3.1

Negative Habits, Patterns, and Beliefs

Think about some of the limiting beliefs you identified in the Law of Attraction lesson.

What are some patterns or behaviors that you would like to change?

What are some limiting or negative beliefs that you would like to shift to the positive?

What are some habits you would like to let go of?

Lesson 3.2

Resistance vs Allowing

Look at the chart below and think about areas of your life where you may be resisting instead of allowing.

Resistance	Allowing
Based in Ego	Based in Divine
Externally Focused	Internally Focused
Judging and Critical	In the Heart, Accepting
Rigid and Inflexible	Flowing
Fear	Love
Distrusting	Trusting
Blocks and Obstacles	Ease and Effortless
Unworthiness	Worthiness
Energetic Imbalance	Energetic Balance
Closed-Minded	Open-Minded

What areas of your life are you experiencing resistance in?

5 Ways *to Release Resistance:*

1 INCREASE SELF-AWARENESS

Become an observer to your negative beliefs, habits, thoughts and patterns. Notice without judgment how you keep yourself blocked or stuck in certain situations or issues. Stay curious without attachment, like a scientist observing an experiment. Keep a journal and record beliefs and patterns that you notice you play out in your life. Having awareness of your thoughts and behaviors gives you the power to rewire and heal them.

2 STOP THE NEGATIVITY IN ITS TRACKS

As you observe your thoughts and behaviors, especially the ones you want to change, you may notice a desire to shift the way you react. The first step to doing this is to shut it down as soon as you become aware of the negative thought, pattern, habit, or belief by stopping it mid-process. This is how you rewire the brain synapses and neural pathways in your brain. At first, it may feel like you're watching a train wreck happen that you can't stop or control, but with practice you'll find that it gets easier and eventually it becomes second nature. You can do this in a kind manner, firmly but gently. It's like being compassionate with yourself and at the same time setting a solid boundary for your inner critic.

3 FOCUS YOUR ATTENTION ELSEWHERE

When we shift our attention to something else and quit focusing on the struggle, we begin allowing. We're taught to take action, to go out and make things happen. Surrendering and letting go of our attachment to the thing we're resisting feels strange or unproductive. When you find yourself struggling in resistance, focus your attention on something else. Find some things to do that will distract you, perhaps it's time for self-care or enjoying a night out with friends. Getting out of your own way and letting go moves you into a place of allowing, where things flow easily and effortlessly.

4   LET GO OF JUDGMENT

People who have been on the spiritual or healing journey a long time tend to be hard on themselves when they encounter resistance or get stuck. The believe they should have 'known better' or 'done better' but they're still stuck, and they've made it worse by going into judgment and shame about it. We all get stuck. It happens. The key is being able to accept that's where you're at, and then willing to do what's needed to begin gaining some forward momentum again.

5   UNCOVER WHAT'S BENEATH THE RESISTANCE

You've probably heard the saying, "What we resist, persists". Getting unstuck requires moving through the fear, and resistance is just a signal from your subconscious that you've gotten close to a sensitive issue. An underlying thought, pattern, or belief that's trying to protect you from what it perceives as life-threatening danger. Try not to be too harsh with yourself when you experience resistance, it's just an indication to pay attention so that you can identify what's going on under the surface, and then you can move through it.

Some things I can do to release resistance are:

Observe your thoughts over the course of a day and keep track of the negative ones. Make a mark every time you have a negative thought and then write about your observations.

Use this space here to track your negative thoughts:

Observations from tracking my thoughts:

Lesson 3.3

Using Mantras in Your Daily Practice

"A mantra is not just something to chant. It is not chanting. A mantra is something to let sink deep in your being, just as roots go deep into the earth. The deeper the roots go into the earth, the higher the tree will go into the sky."

—Osho

Saying mantras is a great way to help with a busy mind, looping or obsessive/anxious thoughts, or when negativity hits. Mantras calm and center the mind and help relieve symptoms of anxiety, stress, and depression. A mantra is usually a Sanskrit word, phrase, or sound that is repeated in a mindful or meditative way. Mantras are often repeated 108 times, which is a sacred number in Hinduism and yogic traditions.

Here are some examples of mantras you can use:

- *Om Gum Ganapatayei Namaha* (Removing of Obstacles)

- *Om Shanti Om* (Peace)

- *Om Shree Dhanvantre Namaha* (Healing)

- *Om Namo Bhagavate Vasudevaya* (Liberation)

- *Om Radha Krishnaya Namaha* (Joy & Bliss)

- *Om Shreem Mahalakshmiyei* Namaha(Abundance)

- *Om Kama Pujitayei Namaha* (Sacred Love Making)

Lesson 3.4

Observing is a great technique to use if you have a hypercritical mind, chronic toxic shame, or perfectionistic tendencies. It allows you to step outside of the thought patterns of "not good enough" so that you can investigate where the belief originates from and challenge it in a compassionate way.

1 Set the intention that you want to develop awareness of your negative thought patterns and limiting beliefs.

2 Start paying attention throughout the day as they crop up for you, and as you notice what is happening, shift into the observer/scientist mind.

3 Be curious about the thoughts you're aware of and notice if there are any sensations anywhere in your body that are connected to the thoughts.

4 Observe aloud or in your head something like, "Well, isn't it interesting that I'm thinking about _____ and I'm experiencing _____ in my body." Or, "How interesting that I tend to _____ when I'm thinking about _____."

5 Get to the belief underneath the thoughts, by adding, "Where is this thought coming from?" or "I wonder where the root of this thought pattern is" and wait for the response.

6 Record the observations and then notice patterns or behaviors that are associated with the thoughts.

Notes from Observing practice:

Lesson 3.5

Gratitude and Appreciation are quick and easy ways to shift a negative mindset to the positive.

Write a list of 10 things you are grateful for:

One of the easiest ways is to write down a list of ten things you are grateful for each night and then read them aloud before you go to sleep. This allows you to bring a positive vibration and thought momentum in your dream state.

1. _____
2. _____
3. _____
4. _____
5. _____
6. _____
7. _____
8. _____
9. _____
10. _____

Three Good Things

A variation of the exercise above is to spend 5-10 minutes each evening writing down in detail about three good things that happened to you that day, whether they were big or little, and describing why you think they happened.

1. _____
2. _____
3. _____

_____   50

GRATITUDE VISUALIZATION

Another gratitude practice you can do is to sit quietly in a comfortable position and think about what you are grateful for. Gently close your eyes and imagine the people, places, things, situations, and events that warm your heart, bring you joy, or that you greatly cherish. Sit in that feeling for 5-10 minutes. You can add an extra layer of gratitude by saying thank you for each of those things you are grateful for in your life, and then allow that feeling to wash over you and flow through you and all around you. When you are ready, open your eyes and bring your awareness back into the room.

WRITE A GRATITUDE LETTER

Spend some time composing a letter for something which you are grateful about. It can be to a person, but it doesn't have to be. You can write gratitude letters to the earth and the angels, your body, future self, and to addictive substances. The possibilities are endless, just pick whatever you feel you need to express some gratitude and start writing.

Dear _____,

_____
_____
_____
_____
_____
_____
_____
_____
_____
_____
_____
_____
_____
_____
_____
_____

Lesson 3.6

Guided Meditation

Guided meditations are great to begin with because you can just sit or lie down while listening to someone else guiding you through the meditation, and it gives your mind something to focus on. Listening to someone else's voice in meditation, just like what would occur in a hypnotherapy session, provides a distraction for the conscious mind so that healing can take place under the surface in the subconscious mind.

Guided meditations come in many different formats and cover a variety of topics from relaxation to healing to spiritual journeys. You may find as you try out different guided meditations that you like some people's voices, or music, or style better than others. I have a couple of dozen of my favorites and rotate what I listen to depending on my mood or needs at the time.

Listen to the guided meditations in the free Supplemental Materials portal at overcomingtrauma.allisonsmiley.com.

Don't ever let anyone dull your Sparkle

Lesson 4.1

People often use spiritual bypassing to avoid dealing with painful issues. This can create problems down the road when the underlying issues have not been addressed

Spiritual Bypassing Quiz:

Do you tend to focus on helping other people heal or overcome issues?

Are you involved in support groups or communities (ie: 12 Step, church, etc) where being of service takes a lot of your time?

Do you find that you don't have any extra time to take care of yourself because you are busy helping or taking care of others?

Are you focusing on a significant others' issues - looking for solutions for their problems or asking them to get help?

Are you using positive affirmations, manifesting/The Secret, or other spiritual tools to avoid dealing with your trauma issues?

Do you find yourself so busy from helping others or your commitments to service that you have no time to think about your own 'stuff'?

Do you avoid talking about your feelings or trauma issues because you are trying to 'stay positive'?

Are you aware that there are things you need to feel and process but keep putting it off or distracting yourself with spirituality or helping others?

Do you use astrology, psychic readings, or energy reports to explain away your moods or behaviors instead of accepting them as they are?

Do you buy a lot of self-help books, attend classes or retreats, or follow spiritual gurus searching for the answer to feeling better?

Some thoughts as I reflect on these questions:

Lesson 4.2

Feel and Heal Process

Begin by getting into a comfortable position, either seated or lying down. Take in some nice, deep relaxing breaths and follow the steps below.

1 INVOKE MINDFUL AWARENESS OR SACRED PRESENCE

If you've been practicing mindfulness, take a moment to get centered and grounded, and shift your awareness into the present moment. You can also call in the divine or sacred presence (whatever that is for you) and surround yourself in a cocoon of divine white light and protection. Feel the white light flowing through you and all around you, feeling safe and secure and protected.

2 IDENTIFY THE FEELING/EMOTION

As you sit for a few moments, become aware of what the feeling or emotion is that you are experiencing. You can say it out loud or in your head. If you are connecting to a feeling in your body such as exhaustion or hunger or pain, what would this translate into if they were an emotion or feeling?

3 SENSE THE FEELING/EMOTION IN YOUR BODY

Once you've identified what the feeling or emotion is, notice where you are experiencing it in your body. Is it a knot in your belly, a tightness in your chest, a lump in your throat? Give yourself a few moments to become aware of where the feeling is in your body and just notice it without judgment.

4 SIT WITH THE FEELING/EMOTION

Take some time to sit with the feeling or emotion. Allow yourself to really feel it in your body. There may be some discomfort at first but give yourself some time to allow it to come to the surface so it can be released and let go

5 ACCEPT IT

Acknowledge the feeling or emotion you're experiencing. You might like to investigate a little further and ask what you can learn from it or how you can grow from the situation or experience.

6 REFRAME IT

Sometimes a memory comes up when we are processing emotions, particularly when we tune into the sensations in the body. Because our bodies hold trauma and memories, they may come to the surface while we go through the process. Think about how you could re-write or reframe the outcome. Was there something that needed to be said that you weren't allowed or able to say at the time? Was there something you needed in the situation like a supportive friend or someone there to help you? Did you need to take some type of action like remove yourself from the situation or stand up for yourself? Take a few minutes to reframe the memory with what you needed at that time. Really feel the shift take place from feeling powerless or like a victim to feeling strong and fully supported and protected by the divine

7 RELEASE IT

Now, with gratitude for the lesson and healing, take a few deep, calming breaths and allow yourself to release and let it go. Allow it to come to the surface, flowing out of your body and away from you, sending it into the Violet Flame to be transmuted and transformed. Or you can visualize it floating down a stream or river until it completely disappears. Take as much time as you need until the process feels complete

8 REPEAT IF NEEDED

Sometimes when we go through this process, there are underlying emotions beneath the feeling or emotions we just released. If this happens, go back to Step 1 and begin the process again so that you can release the underlying emotion as well. Anger may be an initial emotion that covers up hurt or sadness, or that worry/anxiety may cover up fear or shame. As you continue to work through the Feel and Heal process, you'll notice it gets easier and more comfortable with consistent practice.

Notes:

Practice: Feel and Heal Process

The idea of intentionally feeling an emotion that in the past we may have gone to great lengths to avoid feeling can seem daunting or overwhelming. Negative emotions are just signal that something within us is not in alignment with Love, our true state of being. They are guiding us to this misalignment so that we can identify it, process it, heal it, and let it go.

INVOKE MINDFUL AWARENESS OR SACRED PRESENCE:

Ways I can use mindfulness or sacred presence for this practice:

_____
_____
_____
_____

IDENTIFY THE EMOTION:

If you are connecting to a feeling in your body such as exhaustion or hunger...what would this translate into if they were an emotion?

_____
_____
_____
_____

SENSE THE EMOTION IN YOUR BODY: (RELEASES FROM PHYSICAL BODY)

After you identify what the emotion is, notice where you are experiencing it in your body (can be in multiple places) – tightness in the chest, lump in your throat, knot in your belly:

_____
_____
_____
_____

SIT WITH THE EMOTION: (RELEASES FROM MENTAL BODY)

Allow yourself to really feel it in your body. There may be some discomfort at first but allow it to come to the surface so it can be released and let go. Acknowledge the fear, become aware of any memories coming up.

_____
_____
_____
_____

ACCEPT IT: (RELEASES FROM EMOTIONAL BODY)

Acknowledge the feeling or emotion you're experiencing. Ask what you can learn from it or how you can grow from the situation or experience.

_____

_____

_____

_____

RESCRIPT OR REFRAME IT: (RELEASES FROM SPIRITUAL BODY)

What did you need at that time? Really feel the shift take place from feeling powerless to feeling strong and fully supported, loved, and protected.

_____

_____

_____

_____

RELEASE IT:

With gratitude for the lesson and healing, take a few deep calming breaths and allow yourself to release and let it go. Take as much time as you need until the process feels complete.

_____

_____

_____

_____

REPEAT IF NEEDED:

Sometimes there are underlying emotions beneath the one we just released. Go back to Step 1 to release the underlying emotion as well. For example, anger may cover up hurt or sadness, worry/anxiety may cover up fear or shame.

_____

_____

_____

_____

***IT MAY HELP TO USE THE _WHERE IS MY IMBALANCE_ WORKSHEETS FROM PAGES 31-35.

Lesson 4.3

Journaling to Process Emotions

Find a comfortable, quiet, and private space where you can take some time to record your thoughts, feelings, or experiences. You can use any kind of notebook or paper, nothing fancy is required for this exercise.

Here are some tips for beginning (or restarting) a daily journaling practice:

1. If you are concerned about getting too deep into your feelings, set a timer for a few minutes to start with and then see how things are going. If you are doing well, set the timer again for a few more minutes. If you are struggling and feel like you might get sucked under with too much emotion, shift your focus to positive affirmations or a gratitude list. Revisit the topic another time.

2. Write about challenging or triggering events in the third person.

3. Before beginning the journaling practice, imagine that you are surrounded by divine white light or a ball of pink divine love. Know that you are fully loved, supported, and protected as you go through this writing process.

4. If you are feeling stuck with what to write about, start writing your thoughts in the moment. That might even begin with "I don't know what to write about but I know Allison said that journaling is supposed to be a great practice for self-care and so I'm giving it a shot even though I'm not quite sure what I think or feel about it right now." It is OK to ramble on. Keep going without judgment or worrying about what is being written down. Pretty soon the words will begin flowing in a more confident and natural style for you.

5   Be honest. There is no need to worry about what people think or trying to look your best and appearing perfect on paper. This is just for you and your personal growth and development.

6   Write about your goals and dreams. Give yourself permission to think big and really go for it.

7   Journal daily. A consistent practice of writing down your thoughts and feelings has tremendously positive benefits and can create huge shifts in your self-awareness, intuition, and overall emotional well-being

Some thoughts I have about Journaling:

Lesson 4.4

If you struggle with feelings of not being good enough, self-loathing, or dislike certain aspects of yourself, self-esteem affirmations are an effective practice to rewire the neural pathways in your brain to create new, positive thoughts and beliefs about yourself and your life.

- Today I am capable of handling anything that happens.

- I am attracting great things into my life.

- I am confident and strong.

- I am supported by the universe.

- I feel good about who I am.

- I am a unique and priceless person.

- My life is wonderful.

- I love myself.

- I am a happy, positive person.

- I am worthy.

- I'm capable of creating and maintaining a great life.

- I deserve to have a great life.

- I am beautiful inside and out.

- I'm capable of changing my life for the better.

- I deserve to have a great life.

- I am a divine being of light.

- My family loves and supports me.

- My friends are always there for me.

- I am creative and interesting.

- I am perfect just the way I am.

- I can change my life story whenever I want.

- I have the right to change my life to suit my personal needs.

- The movies in my mind are wonderful because I choose to make them so.

- Today I am taking steps toward a happier life.

- I have a wonderful circle of friends.

- I am a caring person with lots of friends who care about me.

- I accept myself for who I am.

- I can trust and rely on myself.

- I am unconditionally loved by the universe.

- I am fully competent and capable.

- I honor and respect myself.

- My worth as a human being is unconditional.

- I am respected and well-liked by all the people that I know.

- I accept and rejoice at my individuality.

- I respect myself, I respect others, and others respect me.

- I trust myself completely.

- People like to be around me.

- I create my own reality.

- I can say no to other people.

- I have healthy personal boundaries.

- Everyone is special, including me.

- It is OK for me to be good to myself.

- I can put myself first without feeling guilty.

- If I need something, it is OK to give it to myself.

- I have the right to be happy and healthy.

- I spend time in meaningful ways.

- My relationship with my family is better than ever.

- I forgive myself and look forward to the future.

- Others value me just for being who I am.

- All of my dreams are coming true.

- Today I treat myself like a queen.

- What matters most is what I think about myself.

- I live my life according to my own beliefs and values.

- Other people honor and appreciate who I truly am inside.

- I am my own best friend.

- I listen to myself and I trust myself.

- I accept myself.

Lesson 4.5

Practicing self-compassion helps us silence the inner critic and develop a kind and accepting attitude toward ourselves.

What are some ways that I can let go of self-criticism and practice kindness toward myself?

What are some ways that I can silence the inner critic and offer support and encouragement instead?

Identify some practices for reducing negative thought patterns and behaviors and increase self-awareness that supports positive change?

68

Lesson 4.6

Radical acceptance helps with letting go and moving on and brings freedom and peace to your life. When we completely and totally accept something exactly the way it is right now, we are no longer giving it our energy or trying to control it. This process frees us from powerlessness and victim mentality. We become empowered by radically accepting ourselves and our lives with a kind and compassionate heart

What are some areas of your life that you might be resisting or fighting reality?

What are some situations or events you may be bitter or resentful about?

What are some ways you may try to control situations or behaviors of others or expect other people to change to make you happy?

Radical Acceptance Practice

Now that you have an awareness of areas you may be resisting, shift your focus to acceptance.

1 Begin by taking in some calm, relaxing breaths. Breathing peace and calm into your heart. Say to yourself or out loud, "I am willing to accept".

2 Then, notice any tension or tightness that you might be holding in your body and continue breathing peace and calm into your heart, sending it throughout your entire body.

3 Continue saying to yourself or out loud, "I am willing to accept myself, my life, and these situations exactly as they are" until you feel your body relax and let go.

4 When you are ready, bring your awareness back into the room and open your eyes. Repeat this practice as often as you need to.

What I noticed during this exercise:

10 Steps to Practicing Radical Forgiveness

Radical acceptance helps with letting go and moving on and brings freedom and peace to your life. When we completely and totally accept something exactly the way it is right now, we are no longer giving it our energy or trying to control it.

1 Observe that you are questioning or fighting reality ("it shouldn't be this way").

2 Remind yourself that the unpleasant reality is just as it is and cannot be changed ("this is what happened").

3 Remind yourself that there are causes for the reality ("this is how things happened").

4 Practice accepting with your whole self (mind, body, spirit) - Use accepting self-talk, relaxation techniques, mindfulness and/or imagery.

5 List all of the behaviors you would engage in if you did accept the facts and then engage in those behaviors as if you have already accepted the facts.

6 Imagine, in your mind's eye, believing what you do not want to accept and rehearse in your mind what you would do if you accepted what seems unacceptable.

7 Attend to body sensations as you think about what you need to accept.

8 Allow disappointment, sadness or grief to arise within you.

9 Acknowledge that life can be worth living even when there is pain.

10 Do pros and cons if you find yourself resisting practicing acceptance.

"You're off to great places, today is your day. Your mountain is waiting, so get on your way."

- Dr. Suess

Notes:

MODULE 5

MOVING INTO THE HEART

Lesson 5.1

Living from the Heart

"If we want there to be peace in the world, we have to be brave enough to soften what is rigid in our hearts, to find the soft spot and stay with it. We have to have that kind of courage and take that kind of responsibility. That's the true practice of peace."

– Pema Chodron

Living from the Heart completely transforms our lives - improving the way we live, love, parent, and lead.

Review the **10 Guideposts for Wholehearted Living** by Brene' Brown. One a scale of 1-10, notice where you are at for each of the guideposts.

	1	2	3	4	5	6	7	8	9	10
Letting go of What People Think:	○	○	○	○	○	○	○	○	○	○
Letting go of Perfectionism:	○	○	○	○	○	○	○	○	○	○
Letting go of Numbing and Powerlessness:	○	○	○	○	○	○	○	○	○	○
Letting go of Scarcity and Fear of the Dark:	○	○	○	○	○	○	○	○	○	○
Letting go of the Need for Certainty:	○	○	○	○	○	○	○	○	○	○
Letting go of Comparison:	○	○	○	○	○	○	○	○	○	○
Letting go of Exhaustion as a Status Symbol and Productivity as Self-Worth:	○	○	○	○	○	○	○	○	○	○
Letting go of Anxiety as a Lifestyle:	○	○	○	○	○	○	○	○	○	○
Letting go of Self-Doubt and "Supposed to":	○	○	○	○	○	○	○	○	○	○
Letting go of Being Cool and "Always in Control:	○	○	○	○	○	○	○	○	○	○

Notes / Observations:

_____
_____
_____
_____
_____
_____
_____
_____
_____
_____
_____
_____
_____
_____
_____
_____
_____
_____
_____
_____
_____
_____
_____
_____
_____
_____
_____
_____
_____
_____
_____
_____
_____
_____

10 Guideposts for
Wholehearted Living
From Brene Brown's book "The Gifts of Imperfection"

Letting go of...	Cultivating...
What people think	AUTHENTICITY
Perfectionism	SELF COMPASSION
Numbing and Powerlessness	A RESILIENT SPIRIT
Scarcity & fear of the dark	GRATITUDE & JOY
The need for certainty	INTUITION AND TRUSTING FAITH
Comparison	CREATIVITY
Exhaustion as a power symbol & productivity as self-worth	PLAY & REST
Anxiety as a lifestyle	CALM & STILLNESS
Self-doubt & "supposed to"	MEANINGFUL WORK
Being cool & "always in control"	LAUGHTER, SONG & DANCE

"True belonging doesn't require you to change who you are. It requires you to be who you are."

— Brene' Brown

Place people in the circles based on how close you allow them to you.

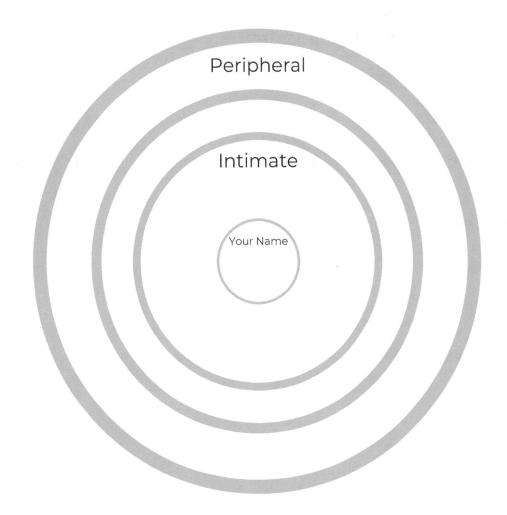

Peripheral

Intimate

Your Name

Your Social Relationship Network

- **Family of Origin** – Family you were raised in.
- **Immediate Family** – Family you currently live with or support actively and regularly.
- **Family of Choice** – Family that you interact with for intimate emotional support (may or may not be biologically related).
- **Friends and social contacts** – Superficial emotional support and casual contact.

Lesson 5.2

HeartMath: Coherent Breathing

Coherent breathing is a tool you can use to connect your breath with your heart. It's great for reducing stress, fear, anxiety, and calming the mind and nervous system.

Coherent Breathing Technique:

1 Connect with your breath in the Heart.

2 Start 5 Second Breathing: Breathe in for 5 seconds, breathe out for 5 seconds.

3 Activate a positive Heart-based emotion: care, appreciation, gratitude, or love.

Observations on using this breathing technique for getting heart-centered:

How would your life change if you could approach your relationships from the Heart?

Which relationships would benefit the most?

How would your life change if you could connect with yourself from the Heart?

Living and Loving from the Heart requires coming from a place of worthiness. Understanding that while you are imperfect and vulnerable, you are also brave and worthy of love and belonging.

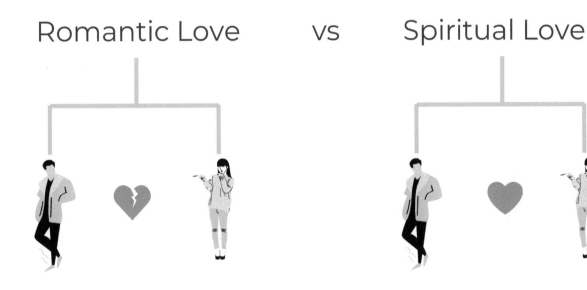

Romantic Love   vs   Spiritual Love

Conditional Love

Based on overcoming deficiencies

Limited

Source Love

Based on inherent worthiness

Unlimited

How have you confused Romantic Love for Spiritual Love?

Cultivating Self-Love: Notice unloving thoughts, breathe into the heart, see yourself from the Heart, from a divine perspective, choose to move into love and acceptance, and honor your journey.

Notes/Observations:

_____
_____
_____
_____
_____
_____

Cultivating Self-Connection: Notice unloving thoughts, breathe into the heart, see yourself from the Heart, from a divine perspective, try on the feeling of self-acceptance, choose to love yourself in imperfection.

Notes/Observations:

_____
_____
_____
_____
_____
_____

Ways to Access the Heart:

- Breathe into the Heart/Coherent Breathing
- Meditative Flow Yoga (Module 1)
- Heart Mantras
- Meditation Journey into the Heart
- Ask the Heart
- Forgiveness (Module 6)

Journal about your experience as you begin to move from Ego/Projecting to Heart-based interactions with yourself and others. Notice the shift within yourself and with those around you.

_____
_____
_____
_____
_____
_____
_____
_____
_____
_____
_____
_____
_____
_____
_____
_____
_____
_____
_____
_____
_____
_____
_____
_____
_____
_____
_____
_____
_____
_____
_____

Lesson 5.3

Tuning into Your Heart's Wisdom

The heart is your own internal GPS system, guiding you to your truth and authenticity. By tapping into the wisdom of your heart, you discover a limitless stream of love, inner wisdom, and compassion for yourself and others.

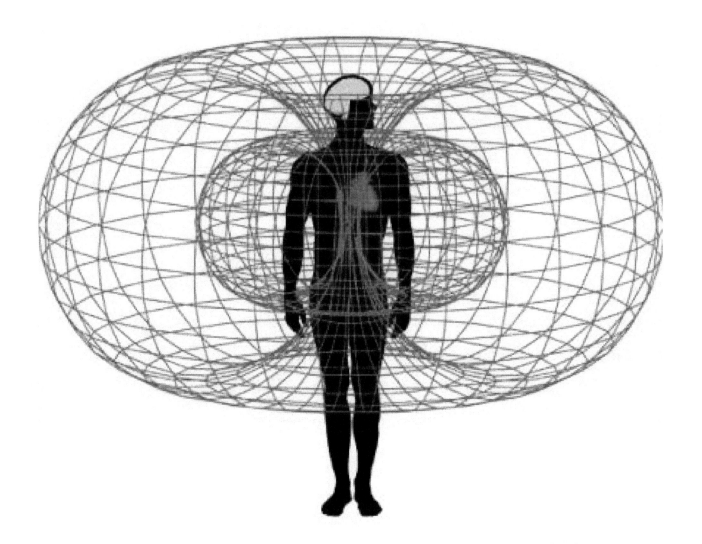

The heart is about 100,000 times stronger electrically and up to 5,000 times stronger magnetically than the brain. More information is sent to the brain from the heart than the other way around

Ask Your Heart Practice:

Place your hands on your chest over your heart and gently close your eyes. Take in some nice deep, relaxing, and calming breaths.

Tune in to the energy of your heart and visualize a pink light surround your heart. Allow this pink light to expand, flowing through you and all around you, until the pink light is completely surrounding you.

As you inhale, breathe in pink light into your heart, and exhale it out into your energy field. When you feel centered in the sacred space of the heart, ask your heart a clear, direct question (or questions).

Wait for the answer to come. Take all the time you need here.

Once you feel you received the guidance from your heart, move your hands into prayer position at your heart and thank your heart for the love, guidance, and wisdom it shared with you.

Slowly bring your awareness back into your body and back to the room.

NOTES:

_____
_____
_____
_____
_____
_____
_____
_____
_____
_____
_____
_____
_____
_____
_____

Lesson 5.4

As we know from Module 3, using mantras is a great way to shift negativity and get out of your head/ego. Heart mantras help you drop into your heart space and allow you to shift out of fear, anxiety, and worry and move into a calm, loving, and peaceful state

Repeat these mantras 108 times

Aham Prema:
Pronounced: A-ham Pray-ma
Translation: I AM Divine Love

How does this mantra feel in your heart?

Om Namo Bhagavate Vasudevaya
Pronounced: Om na-moe Ba-ga-va-tay Va-soo-day-vie-ya
Translation: I bow to the Divine who lives in the hearts of all

How does this mantra feel in your heart?

Lesson 5.5

Journey into the Heart

Listen to the Journey into the Heart meditation in the Supplemental Materials.

Notes from my Journey into the Heart:

Lesson 5.6

Gratitude and Appreciation

Gratitude has been shown to reduce depression and anxiety, increase relationship satisfaction, and increase resilience in times of stress or difficult situations. It is literally impossible to complain and be grateful at the same time!

Gratitude and Appreciation are quick and simple ways to move into your heart and shift from negativity to wholeheartedness.

5 things I am Grateful for today:

I Appreciate my life because:

I Appreciate myself because:

I Am Grateful for these people in my life:

I Appreciate them because:

I Appreciate my body for being:

I am Grateful for my body because:

3 AMAZING things that happened today:

How does living in my heart affect my relationships with others?

Be so happy that, when other people look at you, they become happy too.

Notes/Observations from this Module:

_____
_____
_____
_____
_____
_____
_____
_____
_____
_____
_____
_____
_____
_____
_____
_____
_____
_____
_____
_____
_____
_____
_____
_____
_____
_____
_____
_____
_____
_____

MODULE 6

FORGIVENESS AND LETTING GO

What is Forgiveness

Most people misunderstand the concept of forgiveness. We think that if we forgive and let go, that we somehow condone or approve of the actions of others.

Or we take the "holier than thou" approach and think when we forgive someone that we are somehow better than them because they are the ones who messed up and we have decided to gift them with our forgiveness.

We might also forgive someone out of a sense of obligation because it's what we're taught or it's the spiritual thing to do.

Finally, there is the illusion of forgiveness by pretending we are not angry or upset, or by making excuses for someone like "they didn't know better" or "they did the best they could."

What Forgiveness is NOT

1. Forgiving by pretending we are not upset or angry
2. By forgiving someone, we condone their actions or behaviors
3. "Bestowing" forgiveness on someone
4. Forgiving by making excuses for someone's actions or behaviors
5. Forgiving because it is the right thing to do

These versions of forgiveness are not authentic and do not provide any real sense of relief from the pain, hurt, or anger we experienced from the event or situation. We must commit to the process of truly forgiving and letting go or it will just continue to cause suffering for us.

Am I ready to let go and forgive those who hurt me?

Am I ready to let go and forgive myself?

Am I ready to take my energy and power back?

How would my life change if I finally let these things go?

Which relationships would improve through forgiveness?

How would the relationship with myself improve with forgiveness?

Benefits of Forgiving

Forgiveness is loving yourself enough to take your energy and your power back. It is never about the other person. It is about letting go, healing, and moving on in your life in a positive way.

By forgiving those who have hurt us, we are essentially clearing the way so we can finally experience the joy and beauty of living with improved health, mental clarity, passion, purpose, and peace of mind.

12 Benefits of Forgiving

Healthier relationships

Improved mental health

Less anxiety, stress, and hostility

Lower blood pressure

Fewer symptoms of depression

A stronger immune system

Improved heart health

Improved self-esteem

Setting better boundaries for yourself and others

Increase in understanding, compassion, and empathy

Increase in kindness toward self

Fewer triggers and knee-jerk reactions

Lesson 6.2

This is a powerful ancient Hawaiian forgiveness process. The Hawaiian word ho'oponopono comes from ho'o (to make) and pono (right). The repetition of the word pono means "doubly right" or being right with both self and others.

This forgiveness process allows you to disconnect the discordant energy between you and others in a positive, loving way. There are four steps to the practice – repentance, forgiveness, gratitude, and love.

It is such a simple yet powerful tool to use for healing past hurts and letting go of the pain so you can move forward in your life.

Get into a comfortable position in a quiet space. Think of the person, event, or situation that you would like to forgive and heal. If you are not ready to forgive someone just yet, you can keep it general or use it for self-forgiveness.

Begin by repeating these words:

I'm sorry

Please forgive me

Thank you

I love you

Repeat this prayer 108 times like you would with a mantra. It is best to do this for at least 30 days.

Person, event, or situation I need to forgive:

I need to forgive myself for:

Notes/Observations from using Ho'oponopono:

Lesson 6.3

Prayers for Forgiveness

Prayers of forgiveness are an excellent and simple way to shift the energy of the situation and take your power back.

Lineage Prayers

(These prayers were written by Howard Wills)

Lineage prayers are a powerful way to clear ancestral karma and DNA and release family patterns and struggles. The study of epigenetics shows that traumas and unresolved emotions were imprinted onto our parents' and ancestors' nervous systems and are passed down from generation to generation. Generational karma that we receive from our lineage is in our DNA.

Think about your family patterns – alcoholism, depression, abuse, illnesses, money issues, or victim consciousness – all stem from generational karma, our ancestral DNA. By incorporating lineage prayers into our daily practice, we can heal and clear these karmic issues.

Get into a comfortable position in a quiet space. Take some nice, deep relaxing breaths. When you are ready, read the prayers aloud.

Prayer to cleanse relationships with all women:

For all of the women who have ever hurt me, I forgive you, all of you. Mother(s), mother(s)-in-law, daughter(s), daughter(s)-in-law, sister(s), sister(s)-in-law, aunt(s), grandmothers, friends, ex-lover(s)/ex-wife(s), partner(s), wife. I ask that you all please forgive me. Divine Light, please help us all to forgive each other and to forgive ourselves. Let us all forgive and release ourselves for our hurts, wrongs, and mistakes to ourselves and to others. Please, Divine Light. Thanks, Divine Light. Amen.

Prayer to cleanse relationships with all men:

For all of the men who have ever hurt me, I forgive you, all of you. Father(s), father(s)-in-law, son(s), son(s)-in-law, brother(s), brother(s)-in-law, uncle(s), grandfathers, friends, ex-lover(s)/ex-husband(s), partner(s), husband. I ask that you all please forgive me. Divine Light, please help us all to forgive each other and to forgive ourselves. Let us all forgive and release ourselves for our hurts, wrongs, and mistakes to ourselves and to others. Please, Divine Light. Thanks, Divine Light. Amen.

Divine, for me and my entire lineage throughout all time, past, present, and future: please help us all forgive all people, help all people forgive us, and help us all forgive ourselves. Please Divine. Thank you, Divine. Amen.

Buddhist Prayer of Forgiveness:

This prayer is a beautiful reminder that we all do the best we can with the level of awareness that we are at in the moment. We are all imperfectly perfect.

Get into a comfortable position in a quiet space. Take some nice, deep relaxing breaths. When you are ready, read the prayer aloud:

If I have harmed anyone in any way either knowingly or unknowingly through my own confusions,
I ask their forgiveness.

If anyone has harmed me in any way either knowingly or unknowingly through their own confusions,
I forgive them.

And if there is a situation I am not yet ready to forgive,
I forgive myself for that.

For all the ways that I harm myself, negate, doubt, belittle myself, judge or be unkind to myself through my own confusions,
I forgive myself.

Lesson 6.4

- The past is gone and I live only in the present now.

- I live in the moment of now and create my life the way I want it.

- I follow the principle of live and let live.

- As I forgive myself, it becomes easier to forgive others.

- As I follow the path of forgiveness, I can draw my new life plan and move forward as I wish.

- Each day is a new opportunity.

- Today is the first day of my new life free from the past.

- I forgive everyone from my life in the past and love myself into the future.

- I move beyond forgiveness to understanding and I have compassion and kindness for all.

- I am forgiving, loving, gentle and kind.

- I am safe in the knowledge that life loves me.

- I easily forgive others and I am easily forgiven.

- I forgive myself and release my past.

- I forgive and communicate Love, easily and effortlessly now.

- I now liberate my past from my mind, body and spirit. I am free!

- I forgive my family and embrace them with Love and compassion.

- I am deeply loved and forgiven.

- I release the past and look forward to the future.

- My forgiving nature is contagious.

- I set my past free and forgive myself for my participation.

- I am willing to forgive.

- I release myself from my anger and let the past go.

- The past is forgiven and I am thankful.

- I let go of my hurt and anger toward others.

- I allow divine love to permeate my thoughts.

- I live in the now each moment of each day.

- Today, I choose to forgive myself.

- My memory of this situation is healed.

- I move forward with renewed joy toward life.

- Today is graced with the Divine.

- Forgiveness is a gift I give to myself over and over again.

- Forgiveness expands within me to let the past go and open my eyes to the happiness of tomorrow.

- Forgiving my offender is a gift to myself.

- Forgiving allows me to have better relationships with others.

- With forgiveness, I feel happier and more hopeful.

- The rewards of practicing forgiveness are powerful and freeing.

- I acknowledge that I am fully responsible for my long-term attitude and I choose peace.

- I forgive myself for any thoughts or actions that may have harmed myself or others.

- I forgive myself and choose to move forward to be the best version of my self.

- I release any lingering anger, hurt and resentment and set myself free.

- To forgive is to let go of the extra suffering I have imposed on myself and allow the normal cycle of grief to run its course.

- Rather than dwell in the past, I choose to focus on creating a wonderful future.

- As I release the past, I open my eyes to all the good things oming my way.

- I forgive myself for letting my grudges temporarily sidetrack me from appreciating life.

- I come from Love and I allow Love to flow easily into my life.

- I no longer hold on to the need to punish myself or others. I am free.

- I release the past and let it go.

- I choose to be happy and I do this by letting go of the past and living in the present.

- I no longer dwell on what happened in the past. I am safe.

- I deserve all the wonderful things that life has to offer me.

- I think only positive, compassionate thoughts toward myself and others.

- I know that everyone is doing their best, and I let it go.

- I allow joy and happiness to flow to me now, because I deserve it.

- I am a loving child of the Universe, and I deserve peace.

- By living in the present moment, I can create a wonderful future.

- I am unconditionally loved, appreciated, and accepted.

Lesson 6.5

Listen to the Forgive and Let Go meditation in the Supplemental Materials.

Notes from the Forgive and Let Go meditation:

_____
_____
_____
_____
_____
_____
_____
_____
_____
_____
_____
_____
_____
_____
_____
_____
_____
_____
_____
_____
_____
_____
_____
_____
_____
_____
_____
_____
_____
_____

Lesson 6.6

Step 1: The Basics

Who and what needs to be forgiven?
I want to forgive _____ for _____.

What feelings do you have as a result of this issue?
I am upset with you, _____ for _____. Because
of this, I am feeling _____.
Now, let's release them.
I now choose to release my feelings of _____.

Step 2: Acknowledging Yourself

Do you recognize your own feelings without judgment? Yes / Maybe / No / Unsure
Do you take responsibility now for your own feelings? Yes / Maybe / No / Unsure

Step 3: Interpretation

What interpretations might have you made about the situation, that may or may not be real and
imagined?
_____
_____
_____

What negative beliefs have I made up or have been driving my actions?

- [ ] I am not good enough
- [ ] I am always left out
- [ ] People always abandon me
- [ ] It's not safe to speak my true feelings
- [ ] I will never get what I want no matter how hard I try
- [ ] I am alone
- [ ] I can't be loved
- [ ] Other:

Rate your guilt level
from 1-10 (10 being
the highest):

_____

I am blaming myself for:

_____
_____
_____
_____

This situation makes me feel (circle applicable words):

Angry, disappointed, ashamed, weak, sad, depressed, fearful, apathetic, hostile, jealous, isolated, inferior, small, unimportant, forgotten, irritated, sarcastic, frustrated

This situation also makes me feel:

_____
_____
_____

Step 5: Look ahead

After I finish my forgiveness, I hope to feel:

_____
_____
_____

Step 6: Forgiveness

Consider how this situation could have come about to help you grow. How would forgiveness in this situation help you grow as a person?

_____
_____
_____

Consider how this situation could be no one's fault. How does that help you forgive?

_____
_____
_____

Consider how this situation could have a higher perspective or lesson to learn. How would forgiveness in this situation help you shift your perspective or learn from the experience?

_____
_____
_____

I now release my feelings of:

_____
_____
_____

Step 7: Notes

Write a note to the person you are forgiving:

_____
_____
_____
_____
_____
_____
_____
_____
_____
_____
_____
_____
_____
_____
_____
_____
_____
_____
_____

Write a note to yourself:

_____
_____
_____
_____
_____
_____
_____
_____
_____
_____
_____
_____
_____
_____
_____
_____
_____

Lesson 6.7

Step 1: The Basics

I want to forgive myself for:

_____

_____

I have been judging myself and telling myself:

_____

_____

Step 2: Acknowledging Emotions

When I think about myself, I feel (circle applicable words):

Angry, disappointed, ashamed, weak, sad, depressed, fearful, apathetic, hostile, jealous, isolated, inferior, small, unimportant, forgotten, irritated, sarcastic, frustrated. I also feel:

_____

_____

I would rate my self-esteem on a scale of 1-10 (1 being lowest, 10 being highest): _____

Do you recognize your own feelings without judgment? Yes / Maybe / No / Unsure

Step 3: Interpretation

What interpretations might have you made about the situation, that may or may not be real and imagined?

_____

_____

What negative beliefs have I made up or have been driving my actions?

- [ ] I am not good enough
- [ ] I am always left out
- [ ] People always abandon me
- [ ] It's not safe to speak my true feelings
- [ ] I will never get what I want no matter how hard I try
- [ ] I am alone
- [ ] I can't be loved
- [ ] Other:

Rate your guilt level from 1-10 (10 being the highest):

_____

Step 4: Look Ahead

After I finish my self-forgiveness, I hope to feel:

_____

_____

Step 5: Forgiveness

Consider how this situation could have come about to help you grow. How would self-forgiveness in this situation help you grow as a person?

_____

_____

Consider how this situation could be no one's fault. How does that help you forgive?

_____

_____

I release my feelings of:

_____

_____

Step 6: Notes

Write a note to yourself:

_____

_____

_____

_____

_____

_____

_____

_____

_____

_____

_____

_____

_____

_____

_____

_____

_____

_____

_____

Self-care

is an

act of

Self-love.

SELF-LOVE AND SELF-CARE

Lesson 7.1

Superwoman Syndrome is a term that was coined in 1984 by Marjorie Hansen Shaevitz in her book of the same name. Superwoman Syndrome occurs when a woman neglects herself as she strives to achieve perfection in every role she is fulfilling. Juggling career and home, managing a never-ending to-do list, being a loving mother and spouse, fulfilling social obligations, and living up to the expectation to excel in all of these areas comes at a cost – mentally, emotionally, physically, and spiritually.

It is just not feasible to function at this level for any sustained period of time. Studies show that girls as young as 13 can be affected by Superwoman Syndrome. The pressure and stress of trying to be everything to everyone can become dangerous and unhealthy.

Emotional and cognitive symptoms of stress:

- Irritability
- Inability to concentrate
- Memory problems
- Mood swings
- Constant negative thinking
- Emotional outbursts
- Indecisiveness
- Lack of sense of humor

Physical symptoms of stress:

- Muscle tension
- Stomach/abdominal pain
- Muscle spasms or nervous tics
- Unexplained rashes or skin irritations
- Sweating when not physically active
- Butterflies in stomach
- Unable to sleep or excessive sleep
- Shortness of breath

10 Signs You've Got Superwoman Syndrome

	Yes	No
You work (in/out of the home) and you're a caregiver (kids, parents, partner)	○	○
You feel like a failure because you aren't doing everything perfectly at home AND at work	○	○
You stay awake all night thinking about everything you need to do the next day, week, month or year	○	○
Your to-do list is longer than a trip from here to the sun	○	○
You worry that your kids/partner/parent isn't getting enough of your time	○	○
You stay up late cleaning/cooking/packing lunches/ironing because you can't stand the thought of not getting everything done	○	○
You get frustrated with yourself because you CAN'T do it all perfectly	○	○
You say yes to EVERYONE and EVERYTHING because you don't want anyone to judge you	○	○
You're afraid of losing your partner, kids, parents' love if you take time for yourself	○	○
You get physical symptoms (headaches/stomach problems) from all of the stress, worry and guilt	○	○

If you answered YES to at least two or more of these, guess what? You've got Superwoman Syndrome. And that makes you a Superwoman.

Sure, your cape is probably wrinkled, faded and has a few stains and tears, but you still have it. You're still a Superwoman.

You put tons of pressure on yourself to do everything right. You're a perfectionist. You have trouble saying no and don't like disappointing people (so you say yes to everything).

You try to be all things for all people all the time because you feel bad if other people feel bad. And the more you do, the more stressed out you get and put yourself at an increased risk of various physical, emotional and mental health issues.

The best way to stop Superwoman syndrome from stressing you out and creating havoc in your life is to **be kinder to yourself**. You can be kinder to yourself by practicing good self-care. By using the tools and practices daily and loving on yourself a little bit every day.

You can use the *Self-Care Planner* and *Daily Practices Guide and Checklist* to help you plan and track your daily self-care routine.

Lesson 7.2

Planning for Extreme Self-Care

What types of situations, events, or circumstances completely wear me out and require extra downtime afterwards?

Do I have any of those coming up in the near future? What are they?

If yes, what are the dates? Do I need to take time off or plan time to be alone afterwards?

What are some self-care practices that I know I need after these types of events or situations?

Lesson 7.3

AYURVEDA Dosha Types

VATA
Cold
Dry
Mobile
Light
Air (Ether)
Move

PITTA
Hot
Oily
Mobile
Light
Fire (Water)
Transform

KAPHA
Cold
Wet
Steady
Heavy
Earth (Water)
Sustain

AYURVEDA Dosha Qualities

	VATA	PITTA	KAPHA
Body	Thin, tall, small features, long-limbs, dry hair/skin, low stamina	Medium build, muscular, freckled	Large build, padded joints, high endurance
Mind/Emotion	Creative, expressive, inspired, playful	Sharp, strategic, intellectual, clarity	Easy-going, kind, loyal, forgiving, consistent
Digestion	Gas, bloating, constipation	Heartburn, colored, stool, diarrhea	Heavy after eating, undigested stool
Imbalanced Emotion	Worry, anxiety, fearful, overwhelmed, spacey, forgetful, inconsistent	Angry, resentful, jealous, critical, controlling, demanding	Sad, depressed, lethargic, greedy, resistant to change
Other Symptoms of Imbalance	Insomnia Dizzy Pain (neck, back, hip) Nervous system issues Large intestine issues	Infection/Inflammation, Skin rash/acne Migraines Eyes/Liver/Gallbladder Mild-back pain	Head/chest congestion Excess mucous Fluid retention Swelling

Notes/Observations about my Dosha type:

_____

_____

_____

Instructions:

To determine your constitution it is best to fill out the chart twice. First, base your choices on what is most consistent over a long period of your life (your prakruti), then fill it out a second time responding to how you have been feeling more recently (your vikruti). Sometimes it helps to have a friend ask you the questions and fill in the chart for you, as they may have insight (and impartiality) to offer. After finishing the chart each time, add up the number of marks under vata, pitta and kapha.

This will help you discover your own ratio of doshas in your prakruti and vikruti. Most people will have one dosha predominan, a few will have two doshas, approximately equal and even fewer will have two doshas in equal proportion. For instance, if your vikruti shows more pitta than your prakruti, you will want to follow a pitta-soothing regimen to try and bring your vikruti back into balance with your prakruti. If your prakruti and vikruti seem about the same, then you would choose the regimen of your strongest dosha.

Excerpted from *Ayurvedic Cooking for Self-Healing* by Usha and Dr. Lad.

OBSERVATIONS	V P K	VATA	PITTA	KAPHA
Body size Body weight	☐☐☐ ☐☐☐	Slim Low	Medium Medium	Large Overweight
Chin Cheeks Eyes	☐☐☐ ☐☐☐ ☐☐☐	Thin, angular Wrinkled, sunken Small, sunken, dry, active, black, brown, nervous	Tapering Smooth Flat Sharp, bright, gray, green, yellow/red, sensitive light	Rounded, double Rounded, plump Big, beautiful, blue, calm, loving
Nose Lips Teeth	☐☐☐ ☐☐☐ ☐☐☐	Uneven shape deviated septum Dry cracked, black/brown tinge Stick out, big, roomy, thin gums	Long pointed, red nose-tip Red, inflames, yellowish Medium, soft, tender gums	Short rounded, button nose Smooth, oily, pale, whitish Healthy, white, strong gums
Skin Hair	☐☐☐ ☐☐☐	Thin, dry, cold, rough, dark Dry, brown, black, knotted, britle, scarce	Smooth, oily, warm, rosy Straignt, oily, blond, gray, red, bald	Thick, oily, cool, white, pale Thick, curly, oily, wavy, luxuriant
Nails	☐☐☐	Dry, rough, brittle, break easily	Sharp, flexible, pink, lustrous	Thick, oily, smooth, polished
Neck Chest Belly Belly-button Hips Joints	☐☐☐ ☐☐☐ ☐☐☐ ☐☐☐ ☐☐☐ ☐☐☐	Thin, tall Flat, sunken Thin, flat, sunken Small, irregular, herniated Slender, thin Cold, cracking	Medium Moderate Moderate Oval, superficial Moderate Moderate	Big, folded Expanded, round Big, pot-belled Big, deep, round, stretched Heavy, big Large, lubricated
Appetite Digestion Taste Thirst Elimination	☐☐☐ ☐☐☐ ☐☐☐ ☐☐☐ ☐☐☐	Irregular, scanty Irregular, forms gas Sweerm sour, salty Changeable Constipation	Strong, unbearable Quickm causes burning Sweet, bitter, astringent Surplus Loose	Slow but steady Prolonged, forms, mucous, Bitter, pungent, astringent Sparse Thick, oily, sluggish
Physical Activity Mental Activity	☐☐☐ ☐☐☐	Hyperactive Hyperactive	Moderate Moderate	Slow Dull slow
Emotions Faith Intellect Recollection	☐☐☐ ☐☐☐ ☐☐☐ ☐☐☐	Anxiety, fear, uncertainty Variable Quick but faulty response Recent good, remote poor	Anger, hate, jealousy Extremist Accurate response Distinct	Calm, greedy, attachment Consistent Slow, exact Slow and sustained
Dreams Sleep	☐☐☐ ☐☐☐	Quick, active, many, fearful Scanty, broken up, sleeplessness	Fiery, war, violence Little but sound	Lakes, snow, romantic Deep, prolonged
Speech Financial	☐☐☐ ☐☐☐	Rapid, unclear Poor, spends on trifles	Sharp, penetrating Spends money on luxuries	Slow, monotonous Rich, good money preserver
TOTAL				

Ideas for Body Self-Care

Some of these will be review from Module 1, but I felt it important to include here so you will have it all in one place for easy reference.

Epsom Salt Baths:

Taking baths with Epsom salts has tremendous benefits, and I do this at least three to five times a week to soothe, heal, and relax my body. I lived with pain and inflammation for over 15 years, so this was a must-have in my self-care practice. Bathing with Epsom salts, which contain magnesium, provides benefits such as soothing aches and pains, reducing inflammation, relieving stress, relieving constipation, and aiding with more restful sleep.

How to do it:

Pour one to two cups of Epsom salts into your bathwater. You can also put them into the running water if you want them to dissolve more quickly. For extra healing benefits, you can add essential oils to the water such as lavender, chamomile, frankincense, ylang-ylang, and citrus. (Avoid essential oils if you are pregnant, nursing, or for infants under one year of age).

Massage Therapy:

Sure, a little bit of pampering is nice but including massage in your self-care routine can also have positive benefits for your physical body. I have had a monthly membership for massages for the past five years and it has helped me reduce the chronic pain, inflammation, and stress in my body. Other benefits of massage therapy are improved circulation, elimination of toxins, improved flexibility, improved sleep, reduced fatigue, and improved immunity.

How to do it:

Research massage places near you that offer monthly memberships. They usually offer a discounted rate for your first massage so you can try it out and if you like it, you can sign up. Most places do not require contracts and are typically month to month. One thing that is important to keep in mind though, with this membership, is that you need to make an appointment and actually go to it. It is easy to make excuses about being too busy to take time for it. Make the appointment, put it on your calendar, and show up for your hour of self-care.

Body Oiling:

Abhyanga is the Ayurvedic art of massage with healing oils and can be done by a practitioner or by yourself at home. The benefits of body oiling include improved circulation, strength, vision, stamina, softer skin, strengthened body tissues, improved tone and skin appearance, and better sleep.

How to do it:

It is good to apply the oil to your body after using a dry brush. The dry brush preps the skin to receive the oil. Select the type of oil you want to use. Traditional ayurvedic practice recommends certain oils depending on your ayurvedic body constitution – Kapha, Pitta, or Vata. To keep it simple though, coconut oil is typically used in the late spring, summer, and early fall, or for those people who have excess heat in their system, as it has cooling properties. Sesame oil is used in the late fall, winter, and early spring or for people who tend to have more cold in their systems. You can do this practice daily, although you will still receive great benefits from body oiling if done just two to three times a week.

Steps to Perform Self-Abhyanga

1 Brush your skin with a dry brush to remove dead skin, dirt, and debris from its surface as well as prepare the skin's pores for receiving the oil.

2 Warm your oil – you can do this while dry brushing if warming your oil in a pot, or rub the oil between your palms if you are short on time.

3 Gently but firmly, massage your body all over: Begin with the neck, working your way down to your feet. Use long strokes for limbs and short strokes for joints. Don't forget fingers and toes and pay extra attention to the soles of your feet, as they contain all the nerve endings and important marma points, or conjunctions of prana, life force energy.

4 Let the oil sit for 5–10 minutes. Don't skip this step, as abhyanga's deeper benefits depend on the body's absorption of the oil and herbs. It takes a few minutes for the oil to penetrate to the deepest layers of the skin, and several minutes more for it to penetrate the tissues of the internal body. This is an excellent time to prepare some tea or practice some deep breathing.

5 Rinse excess oil with a cool shower on warm days, or a warm shower (but not hot) on cold days. Don't skip this step either, as excess oil will clog the pores.

Get Enough Sleep:

I know this one seems obvious and it gets preached to us constantly from health, beauty, medical, and mindfulness experts. It seems like a no-brainer. Go to bed at a reasonable hour, sleep deeply, and then wake up refreshed and ready for the new day. Unfortunately, this is not the case for approximately 50 to 70 million Americans who suffer from some type of sleep disorder. In 2008, the CDC stated that insufficient sleep is a public health epidemic. Over 70 percent of American adults report insufficient sleep for at least one night a month, and 11 percent report insufficient sleep every night. These are startling, but not surprising, numbers given our fast-paced, high-stress lifestyles that leave little time for rest or relaxation. Our health and well-being depend on good sleep.

Benefits of Getting a Minimum of 8 Hours of Sleep

Reduces stress and cortisol levels

Improves memory

Lowers blood pressure

Improves immune system

Helps with weight loss and maintenance

Reduces risk of type 2 diabetes

Reduces pain and inflammation

Regulates hormones

Increases energy

How to do it:

Individuals who have experienced trauma frequently struggle with sleep issues, which have a detrimental effect on health and well-being. It is especially important for your self-care routine to take the proper steps to get enough sleep each night. Once you have established a nightly routine and your body begins to adjust to a consistent bedtime, so many things will fall into place for you. Getting enough sleep is the foundation from which to build.

Tips for getting a better night's sleep:

- Stick to a sleep schedule of the same bedtime and wake up time, even on the weekends.

- Practice a relaxing bedtime ritual.

- If you have trouble sleeping, avoid naps, especially in the afternoon.

- Exercise daily.

- Design your sleep environment to establish the conditions you need for sleep.

- Sleep on a comfortable mattress and pillows.

- Use bright light to help manage your circadian rhythms.

- Avoid alcohol, cigarettes, and heavy meals in the evening.

- Spend the last hour before bed doing a calming activity.

- Keep work materials, computers, or televisions out of the bedroom.

- Use your bed only for sleep and intimacy to strengthen the association between bed and sleep.

- Record your sleep in a sleep diary to help you better evaluate common patterns or issues you may see with your sleep or sleeping habits.

Body Acceptance and Gratitude:

This is a great practice for your self-care toolbox. It can be challenging to go from self-loathing, constantly at war with your body, or being frustrated that it isn't as healthy or functioning as well as you would like to unconditional love and acceptance of it. Starting with acceptance, appreciation, and gratitude works wonders in removing resistance and getting more positive results. When we offer our bodies encouragement and love and praise, and honor and respect them, they are happy and have energy, and perform above our expectations. Incorporating body acceptance, appreciation, and gratitude allows us to begin the process of healing the relationship with our bodies and move toward a more loving and peaceful coexistence.

How to do it:

Get in a comfortable position and take in some nice, deep, relaxing breaths. Begin by scanning your body and sending love to any areas of your body that may be feeling discomfort. Then starting with the top of your head, think of ways that you are grateful for each part of your body, until you reach your toes. Include your muscles, organs, nerves, and so on. "I'm grateful for my arms because they allow me to hug my loved ones." You can also thank your body for everything it does for you; feel free to name examples such as beating your heart, breathing, or turning food into fuel. When you are finished, imagine a pink light surrounding your entire body, flowing through you and all around you.

Meditative Flow Yoga:
Review Module 1 Lesson 4

Breathwork:
Review Module 1 Lesson 2

My Self-Care for the Body Plan:

_____
_____
_____
_____
_____
_____
_____
_____
_____
_____
_____
_____
_____
_____
_____
_____
_____
_____
_____
_____
_____
_____
_____
_____

Lesson 7.4

Some of these will be review from Module 3, but I included them here so you will have it all in one place for easy reference.

Take a Break from Social Media:

We all occasionally need some downtime from scrolling through our social media accounts. Too often we compare our lives to others on these platforms and feel like we don't measure up to the standards we see from our virtual perspective. While social media can be a great way to connect and find support and community, it can also generate quite a lot of negativity regarding social and political issues among "friends."

Studies show that too much screen time can negatively affect our mental health, increasing depression and anxiety. Taking some time away from this provides less screen time overall and a reprieve from the drama and time spent scrolling through posts and advertisements. We then have the opportunity to focus on the present moment and spend quality time with the important people in our lives

Tips for Taking a Break from Social Media

- Put your phone down and out of reach.
- Track your social media time and set limits for yourself.
- Turn off notifications.
- Create phone-free zones in your home.
- Schedule social media time.
- Delete social media apps from your phone.
- Catch up with friends or family by calling or meeting in person.
- Find hobbies that you enjoy and keep your mind off your phone.
- Get out in nature and leave your phone behind.

De-Clutter and Create Sacred Space:

Taking time to get organized and getting rid of items that you no longer need helps with productivity and a positive mindset. When there is an order to your surroundings, it creates a sense of peace and calm, reducing anxiety. It is also easier to find items and makes life run a little more smoothly. When we clear out our closets and donate clothes or household items that we do not need anymore, not only are we helping others who might need those things, but we create space to breathe and think, and for new and positive things to come our way. Holding on to clutter blocks our energy, releasing it opens the flow of energy.

How to do it:

Create a sacred space in your home where you can go to relax and enjoy peaceful time for yourself. Place sacred objects, artwork, statues, incense, candles, pillows, and blankets, or anything else that you find soothing in this space.

Creative Visualization:

The practice of using visualization for desired outcomes is a popular technique used by athletes, business coaches, and law of attraction gurus. Incorporating a daily routine of visualizing your desires as if you are already living them can greatly accelerate the achievement of your goals and dreams. There are several benefits to using visualization: it increases creativity, programs the brain to seek out resources needed to achieve the goal, activates the law of attraction to bring those resources to you, and increases motivation to take action to accomplish your goal.

How to do it:

Get into a comfortable position either lying down or in a chair. Taking some nice, deep, relaxing breaths. Begin to imagine what your life would look like if your goals and dreams had already been achieved. How you would feel, who the people are with you, and the smells or sounds – incorporate this vision as vividly as you possibly can. You can also imagine that you are watching your life play out on a giant movie screen. Once you are finished, bring your awareness back to the room. You can follow this activity up with positive affirmations to help keep you focused on achieving your goals.

Positive Thought Momentum:
Review Module 2 Lesson 3

Mantras:
Review Module 3 Lesson 3

Observing and Rescripting:
Review Module 3 Lesson 4

Guided Meditation:
Review Module 3 Lesson 6

My Self-Care for the Mind Plan:

_____
_____
_____
_____
_____
_____
_____
_____
_____
_____
_____
_____
_____
_____
_____
_____
_____
_____
_____
_____
_____

Ideas for Spirit Self-Care

Some of these will be review from Module 2, but I wanted to include them here so you'll have them all in one place for easy reference.

Spend Time in Nature

Taking the time to be in nature is one of the best gifts you can give yourself. Studies show that spending just 30 minutes in nature has amazing benefits such as improved memory, decreased depression and anxiety, improved concentration, reduced stress, strengthened immune system, and improved overall mood.

How to do it:

Pick a place that calls to you – the beach, the mountains, your local park, a nature trail, or even your backyard. Dedicate the time to really experience the benefits of your surroundings including smells, sounds, and the pleasant feeling of connecting with nature. Plan this time in your schedule each week. Take a quick 30 minutes outside in your neighborhood or make a day trip out of it and venture to a local destination you have been wanting to visit. Better yet, schedule a longer trip to one of your favorite locations to really boost your time in nature and soak up that healing and relaxation.

Get Involved with Community

I have found when working with clients that one of the frequent areas of discontent they experience is feeling disconnected. Practicing self-care for the spirit is a surefire way to reestablish or boost that connection with the divine. In our hectic lives that rely heavily on technology for communication, it is easy to feel isolated and lonely. Joining a community with like-minded people offers that connection and support that is often missing in our lives. Belonging to a spiritual community offers many benefits such as connection to others, support when we are struggling, inspiration, motivation to improve our lives, and a place where we feel safe and secure to be ourselves.

How to do it:

There are a plethora of options to choose from when it comes to spiritual communities, so it is important to be discerning and find one that feels right for you. Meetup is a great resource for finding groups and you can search by the type of group you are looking for. Churches, yoga classes, meditation centers, and spirituality courses are all excellent places to find communities with like-minded people. Once you have found some options that resonate with you, schedule a tour, go to a group meeting, or sign up for a class!

Trust Your Gut:

Intuition is a natural part of our being, but we often second guess ourselves and doubt that "inner voice" when it is telling us something. We have been taught to think and make decisions based on logic, not by what our gut says. As we begin to trust that inner knowing and have success following it on a consistent basis, we build a stronger relationship with ourselves and our divine connection. There are many benefits to trusting your intuition such as gaining confidence in yourself and your decisions, focus and clarity in difficult situations, increased creativity, being more in tune with your physical body, recognizing the messages and nudges when they come to us, and experiencing less fear and worry knowing we are being divinely guided.

How to do it:

Listening to and trusting your intuition is a skill that needs to be developed, so it requires regular practice. As you become aware of a gut feeling or intuitive guidance about something, act on it right away, and continue to do this each time so it feels more comfortable and your confidence continues to grow. Incorporate mindfulness and meditation into your daily practice as they help strengthen intuition. Guidance and messages can come through dreams, so pay attention to your dreams and keep a notepad by your bed to write down any notes or observations from your dreams upon awakening.

Pray and Meditate

It is said that prayer is talking to the divine, and meditation is listening for the response. When we incorporate both practices into our daily self-care routine, we open the lines of communication with the divine going both ways. Prayer and meditation lift our consciousness and align us with our highest selves and the divine. With this connection, we are able to release the pain of the past, trust that we are fully supported by the universe, and move forward with purpose in our lives.

How to do it:

Find a quiet, comfortable space where you can have uninterrupted time for yourself. Take some deep, relaxing breaths and visualize yourself surrounded by a crystalline, divine, white column of light. Begin by saying or reading your prayers. I like to use forgiveness prayers, lineage prayers, gratitude, or the Ho'oponopono prayer. Once you are finished with your prayers, move into the meditation. You can sit in silence, count your breaths, repeat a mantra, or listen to guided meditations, whatever works best for you.

Read or Listen to Uplifting Material

There are so many wonderful inspirational books and audiobooks, videos, podcasts, and music to choose for this self-care practice. I am always reading several books, listening to audiobooks, positive affirmations or music in my car while I'm driving or cleaning the house, and watching motivational videos on YouTube. It is consistently a part of my daily routine and essential for me in maintaining a positive mindset.

How to do it:

Make a list of motivational and inspirational books that you want to read or listen to. You can check them out at the library, read as an e-book, or listen to as an audiobook. Create a collection of uplifting audio recordings such as mantras, spiritual music, podcasts, or positive affirmations. Set aside time to incorporate these into your self-care practice each day.

Chakra Balancing:
Review Module 2 Lesson 6

Violet Flame Meditation:
Review Module 2 Lesson 5

My Self-Care for the Spirit Plan:

_____
_____
_____
_____
_____
_____
_____
_____
_____
_____
_____
_____
_____
_____
_____
_____
_____
_____
_____
_____
_____
_____
_____
_____
_____

Lesson 7.6

Ideas for Emotion Self-Care

Some of these will be review from Module 4, but I wanted to include them here for easy reference.

Self-Esteem Affirmations:

If you struggle with feelings of not being good enough, self-loathing, or dislike certain aspects of yourself, self-esteem affirmations are an effective practice to rewire the neural pathways in your brain to create new, positive thoughts and beliefs about yourself and your life.

How to do it:

Studies show that too much screen time can negatively affect our mental health, increasing depression and anxiety. Taking some time away from this provides less screen time overall and a reprieve from the drama and time spent scrolling through posts and advertisements. We then have the opportunity to focus on the present moment and spend quality time with the important people in our lives

Say No:

Being a people pleaser often means having a difficult time saying no to others when they ask for help. Helping people and being kind, caring, and compassionate is a wonderful trait to have, but everyone has a limit on their time, energy, and how much they can do in a day. People pleasers often overextend themselves and have a hard time setting boundaries for themselves and with others. They often have a fear of rejection and do not want to cause other people to feel hurt or angry. Saying "no" can cause feelings of guilt or regret. On the other hand, not saying "no" enough can cause stress, reduce immune function, and lead to exhaustion and feelings of resentment. It is critically important for our well-being and emotional self-care to set boundaries for ourselves and others.

How to do it:

First, remember that saying no is not rude or selfish. Your self-worth is not tied to how much you do for others. It might help to visualize yourself saying no, especially if it is difficult or uncomfortable for you. See yourself successfully saying no with confidence and kindness, being firm and direct with your response. You can also practice with a friend. It is not necessary to provide reasons or excuses why you are saying no. We often do this because we feel guilty or do not want to hurt other people's feelings. Be honest and sincere. People appreciate and respect a "no" response over someone who agrees out of obligation and ends up resentful about it. The more often you take care of yourself by saying no, the easier it becomes. Once this becomes a comfortable self-care practice for you, you will find that you say yes to things you really want to do, and life becomes much more joyful as a result.

The Benefits of Saying "No"

- **Reduces Stress** – Taking care of others and neglecting your own needs causes anxiety, stress, tension, and exhaustion.

- **Frees up Time** – More time for self-care, family, and activities that you really enjoy.

- **More Energy** – Increased energy and better performance in your work and home life.

- **Eliminates Toxic People in your Life** – People who were only wanting your help or time without reciprocation on their part disappear when they are no longer receiving what they want from you

- **Better Sleep** – Reduced stress, tension, and overtaxing from helping others too much allows for more restful and deeper sleep.

- **Builds Confidence** – Setting proper boundaries for yourself and others sends a message that you are strong and taking care of yourself. The more often you do it, the easier it gets, and the better you feel. Honoring yourself and your needs gains respect from others and often leads to their encouragement and support.

Feel and Heal Process:
Review Module 4 Lesson 2

Journal:
Review Module 4 Lesson 3

Self-Compassion:
Review Module 4 Lesson 5

Radical Acceptance:
Review Module 4 Lesson 6

My Self-Care for the Emotions Plan:

_____
_____
_____
_____
_____
_____
_____
_____
_____
_____
_____
_____
_____
_____
_____
_____
_____
_____
_____
_____
_____

Speak kindly to yourself

Elevate your vibration

Let go of perfection

Focus on the positive

Connect deeply with others

Appreciate what you have

Rest and relaxation

Eat well to nourish yourself

MODULE 8
KEEP MOVING FORWARD

Lesson 8.1

Persistence is the courage to continue moving forward on your healing journey in spite of unexpected setbacks or obstacles.

"The best way out is always through." -- Robert Frost

Hope: What are a few goals you hope to achieve in the future?

Plan & Action: What small actions can you take that will start moving you closer towards these goals?

Believe: Write down 3 affirmation sentences that will help remind you of your capabilities, for instance, "I am capable and resourceful."

Highly persistent people have found ways to keep going despite major setbacks and a lack of evidence that they are moving closer toward their goals. Here are a few qualities that persistent people have in common that keeps them going

- They have a goal or vision that drives or motivates them. They focus on it constantly and devote their energy toward reaching it.

- They have a burning desire to achieve their goal or vision. They use this inner energy and intensity to keep them going.

- They have a strong sense of self and don't let others sway them from their purpose.

- They have highly developed habits (think consistent daily practices or showing up for yourself) which pays off over time.

- They have the ability to adjust and adapt (the message of the dragonfly in my book) through the process.

- They have a support group or people who support their goals and visions. Surrounding ourselves with people who can be there during the tough times helps keep us on track on our healing journey.

- They have a commitment to themselves to achieve their goals and visions. Staying to true to themselves and not compromising on this is crucial in the healing process.

Notes/Observations on the Power of Persistence:

_____
_____
_____
_____
_____
_____
_____
_____
_____
_____
_____
_____
_____
_____
_____
_____
_____
_____
_____
_____
_____
_____
_____
_____
_____
_____
_____
_____
_____
_____
_____

Lesson 8.2

Use this worksheet to get a snapshot of where you were when you started the program and where you are now.

Building Resilience:

I regulate my body/nervous system using the tools and practices

1 ◯ 2 ◯ 3 ◯ 4 ◯ 5 ◯ 6 ◯ 7 ◯ 8 ◯ 9 ◯ 10 ◯

I feel more centered and grounded in my body

1 ◯ 2 ◯ 3 ◯ 4 ◯ 5 ◯ 6 ◯ 7 ◯ 8 ◯ 9 ◯ 10 ◯

I regulate my stress response (4 F's) with tools and practices

1 ◯ 2 ◯ 3 ◯ 4 ◯ 5 ◯ 6 ◯ 7 ◯ 8 ◯ 9 ◯ 10 ◯

I feel safe and at peace in my body

1 ◯ 2 ◯ 3 ◯ 4 ◯ 5 ◯ 6 ◯ 7 ◯ 8 ◯ 9 ◯ 10 ◯

Raising My Vibration:

I use the tools and practices to intentionally raise my vibration

1 ◯ 2 ◯ 3 ◯ 4 ◯ 5 ◯ 6 ◯ 7 ◯ 8 ◯ 9 ◯ 10 ◯

I use the Law of Attraction for healing and setting goals and intentions

1 ◯ 2 ◯ 3 ◯ 4 ◯ 5 ◯ 6 ◯ 7 ◯ 8 ◯ 9 ◯ 10 ◯

I intentionally work my way up the scale of consciousness with the tools and practices

1 ◯ 2 ◯ 3 ◯ 4 ◯ 5 ◯ 6 ◯ 7 ◯ 8 ◯ 9 ◯ 10 ◯

I feel more centered and grounded in my body

1 ◯ 2 ◯ 3 ◯ 4 ◯ 5 ◯ 6 ◯ 7 ◯ 8 ◯ 9 ◯ 10 ◯

Managing My Thoughts:

I shift mind looping and negative thought patterns with the tools and practices

1 ◯ 2 ◯ 3 ◯ 4 ◯ 5 ◯ 6 ◯ 7 ◯ 8 ◯ 9 ◯ 10 ◯

I am feeling less anxious

1 ◯ 2 ◯ 3 ◯ 4 ◯ 5 ◯ 6 ◯ 7 ◯ 8 ◯ 9 ◯ 10 ◯

I feel more capable of handling things that come my way

1 ◯ 2 ◯ 3 ◯ 4 ◯ 5 ◯ 6 ◯ 7 ◯ 8 ◯ 9 ◯ 10 ◯

Feeling Leads to Healing:

I feel more comfortable with my emotions

1 ◯ 2 ◯ 3 ◯ 4 ◯ 5 ◯ 6 ◯ 7 ◯ 8 ◯ 9 ◯ 10 ◯

I am more kind and gentle with myself

1 ◯ 2 ◯ 3 ◯ 4 ◯ 5 ◯ 6 ◯ 7 ◯ 8 ◯ 9 ◯ 10 ◯

I accept situations and events as they are

1 ◯ 2 ◯ 3 ◯ 4 ◯ 5 ◯ 6 ◯ 7 ◯ 8 ◯ 9 ◯ 10 ◯

Moving into the Heart:

I am living more wholeheartedly

1 ◯ 2 ◯ 3 ◯ 4 ◯ 5 ◯ 6 ◯ 7 ◯ 8 ◯ 9 ◯ 10 ◯

I trust the wisdom and guidance of my heart

1 ◯ 2 ◯ 3 ◯ 4 ◯ 5 ◯ 6 ◯ 7 ◯ 8 ◯ 9 ◯ 10 ◯

I have gratitude and appreciation for myself and my life

1 ◯ 2 ◯ 3 ◯ 4 ◯ 5 ◯ 6 ◯ 7 ◯ 8 ◯ 9 ◯ 10 ◯

Forgiveness and Letting Go:

I am more open and willing to forgive and let go

1 ◯ 2 ◯ 3 ◯ 4 ◯ 5 ◯ 6 ◯ 7 ◯ 8 ◯ 9 ◯ 10 ◯

I have released resentments and taken more of my power back

1 ◯ 2 ◯ 3 ◯ 4 ◯ 5 ◯ 6 ◯ 7 ◯ 8 ◯ 9 ◯ 10 ◯

I consistently use tools for forgiveness in my daily practices

1 ◯ 2 ◯ 3 ◯ 4 ◯ 5 ◯ 6 ◯ 7 ◯ 8 ◯ 9 ◯ 10 ◯

Self-Love and Self-Care:

I make self-care a high priority in my life

1 ◯ 2 ◯ 3 ◯ 4 ◯ 5 ◯ 6 ◯ 7 ◯ 8 ◯ 9 ◯ 10 ◯

It is easier to put myself first and take care of my needs

1 ◯ 2 ◯ 3 ◯ 4 ◯ 5 ◯ 6 ◯ 7 ◯ 8 ◯ 9 ◯ 10 ◯

I am learning to practice extreme self-care when needed

1 ◯ 2 ◯ 3 ◯ 4 ◯ 5 ◯ 6 ◯ 7 ◯ 8 ◯ 9 ◯ 10 ◯

Keep Moving Forward:

I am making a commitment to myself to continue my healing journey

1 ◯ 2 ◯ 3 ◯ 4 ◯ 5 ◯ 6 ◯ 7 ◯ 8 ◯ 9 ◯ 10 ◯

I take care of myself even when I am feeling triggered

1 ◯ 2 ◯ 3 ◯ 4 ◯ 5 ◯ 6 ◯ 7 ◯ 8 ◯ 9 ◯ 10 ◯

I am making the tools and practices a priority in my daily routine

1 ◯ 2 ◯ 3 ◯ 4 ◯ 5 ◯ 6 ◯ 7 ◯ 8 ◯ 9 ◯ 10 ◯

Notes/Observations about where I was when I started 8 weeks ago and where I am now:

_____
_____
_____
_____
_____
_____
_____
_____
_____
_____
_____
_____
_____
_____
_____
_____
_____
_____
_____
_____
_____
_____
_____
_____

"If you can't fly then run, if you can't run then walk, if you can't walk then crawl, but whatever you do you have to keep moving forward."

- Martin Luther King Jr

Lesson 8.3

We all know that writing out our goals and intentions helps us get clear on what we want and track our progress. Use this worksheet to plan the next steps of your healing journey.

Some of the tools and practices I really enjoyed doing are:

Tools and practices I did not spend much time on, but want to do more of:

Some of the lessons or practices I was resistant to and would like to revisit at a later time:

Things I learned about and want to go deeper into:

Tools and practices I enjoy doing in the morning:

Tools and practices I enjoy doing in the evening:

Tools and practices I enjoy doing anytime:

Best time of day to make time for myself:

Amount of time I am willing/able to set aside for my daily practices:

The people who support me in my healing journey are:

Lesson 8.4

Using the worksheet from the previous lesson, create a daily routine. You can create routines for different time allowances or by the time of the day you want to do them.

DAILY PRACTICE	MORNING/EVENING	☑
		☐
		☐
		☐
		☐
		☐
		☐
		☐
		☐
		☐
		☐
		☐
		☐
		☐
		☐

Examples of Daily
Practice Routines

Here are some examples of different daily practice routines that you can play around with and see what works best for you. I found that some weeks I enjoyed incorporating a lot of yoga into my morning practices, and then other weeks I would do more meditation and mantras and do very little or no yoga.

I believe that we intuitively know what we need, so listen to that inner voice that is guiding you. Create your own routine and trust the process. There is no right or wrong, nothing needs to be done perfectly, and there is no order or amount of time that has to be followed. This is your time dedicated to your self-care and healing, so do what feels good to you and see what happens.

Example Daily Practice Routines:

30-Minute Daily Practice:

Calming Breathwork
7-Minute Meditative Flow Yoga
Ganesh Mantra – Om Gum
Ganapatayei Namaha (Removing of Obstacles)
Ho'oponopono Prayer
Violet Flame Meditation

Energizing Breathwork
Ganesh Mantra
Journey Into the Heart Meditation
Self-Esteem Affirmations

Calming Breathwork
7-Minute Meditative Flow Yoga
Feel and Heal Process
Violet Flame Meditation

40-Minute Daily Practice:

20-Minute Meditative Flow Yoga
Forgiveness Prayers
Destination Vibration
Self-Love Affirmations

Calming Breathwork
Healing Mantra – Om Shree
Dhanvantre Namaha
Positive Thought Momentum
Ho'oponopono Prayer
Deep Relaxation and Healing Meditation

Energizing Breathwork
7-Minute Meditative Flow Yoga
Journey Into the Heart meditation
Ganesh Mantra
Gratitude Journaling

60-Minute Daily Practice:

20-Minute Meditative Flow Yoga
Healing Mantra
Positive Thought Momentum
Feel and Heal Process
Lineage Prayers
Violet Flame Meditation

Calming Breathwork
7-Minute Meditative Flow Yoga
Ganesh Mantra
Destination Vibration
Forgiveness Meditation
Gratitude Journaling

Calming Breathwork
Positive Thought Momentum
Journey Into the Heart Meditation
Radical Acceptance
Forgiveness Prayers

Morning and Evening Routines

If you do not have time or it feels too overwhelming to do everything in one sitting, I have found that breaking the practices up into a couple of time blocks works great. Many of my clients enjoy doing starting and ending their days with a few of the practices. Here are a couple of examples of morning and evening routines. Again, feel free to customize it with the practices that work best for you depending on which areas need the most attention right now.

Morning
20-Minute Meditative Flow Yoga
Ganesh Mantra
Violet Flame Meditation
Self-Esteem Affirmations

Evening
Epsom Salts Bath With Essential Oil
Forgiveness Prayers
Journey Into the Heart Meditation

Morning
Calming Breathwork
7-Minute Meditative Flow Yoga
Heart Mantra
Destination Vibration Meditation

Evening
Body Oiling With Warm Shower
Gratitude
Positive Thought Momentum
Self-Love Affirmations

Morning
Energizing Breathwork
7-Minute Meditative Flow Yoga
Violet Flame Meditation
Body Oiling With Warm Shower

Evening
Ganesh Mantra
Forgiveness Prayers
Chakra Clearing and Balancing Meditation

Lesson 8.5

Putting it all Together

Use this worksheet to make notes regarding your review of where you are at now and your plan for continuing to use the tools and daily practices.

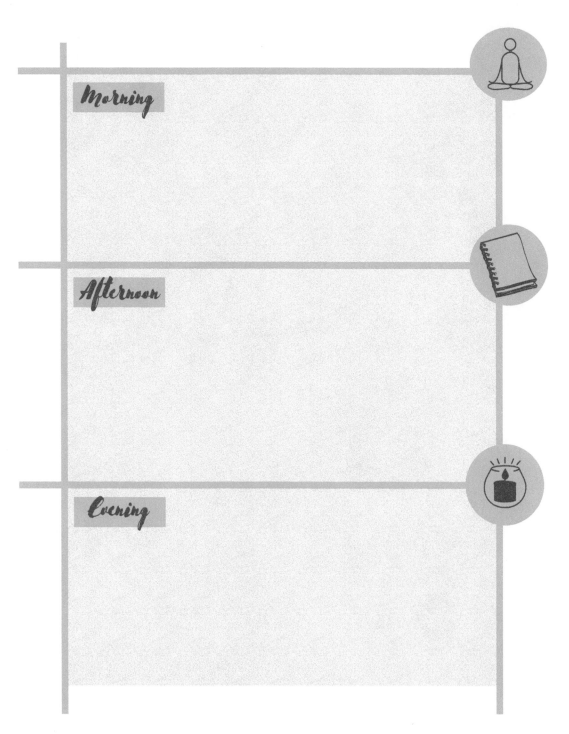

Morning

Afternoon

Evening

My Support Team

We know that it is up to us to take care of our mind, body, spirit and emotions. However, there are days when it helps to have support from those around us. These people can be your family, friends, community members, teachers, colleagues, health professionals, or mentors.

Use this space here to identify your support team.

Who can I call or talk to when I am sad or lonely?

Who celebrates with me when I have good news?

Who am I most happy around?

Who can I be myself around?

Who do I laugh the most with?

Who inspires me?

Who supports my dreams?

Who can I be there for and how?

My Support Team

We know that it is up to us to take care of our mind, body, spirit and emotions. However, there are days when it helps to have support from those around us. These people can be your family, friends, community members, teachers, colleagues, health professionals, or mentors

Use this space here to create a summary of your support team and how they can help you.

Name:_____ Help By: _____ _____ _____ _____	Name:_____ Help By: _____ _____ _____ _____
Name: _____ Help By:_____ _____ _____ _____	Name: _____ Help By: _____ _____ _____ _____
Name: _____ Help By:_____ _____ _____ _____	Name:_____ Help By: _____ _____ _____ _____
Name:_____ Help By:_____ _____ _____ _____	Name:_____ Help By: _____ _____ _____ _____

Yay! I'm so proud of you.

You made it through the 8 Step Method for Healing Trauma, 8-Week Trauma Healing Program.

First, take a moment to honor yourself and your healing journey. It takes a lot of courage to go through the trauma healing process. Plan something special for yourself to recognize your hard work.

Second, keep going back through the materials. Healing is not a linear process and can sometimes be a two steps forward and three back kind of experience. So, revisit these tools as often as you need to and go at a pace that is comfortable for you.

Finally, it's time to celebrate YOU! Watch the video in the Supplemental Materials section to celebrate the amazing transformations you've made throughout the 8 weeks of this program. Take some time to honor your journey and the work that you put in showing up for yourself each week.

Remember to just keep moving forward!

Love and Blessings,

Allison

"A river cuts through rock, not because of its power, but because of its persistence."   – James N. Watkins

Happiness is an Inside Job

References

Ackerman, C. (2020, April 28). 83 Benefits of Journaling for Anxiety, Depression, and Stress. Positive Psychology. https://positivepsychology.com/benefits-of-journaling/

Bonanno, G. A. (2004, January). Loss, trauma, and human resilience: have we underestimated the human capacity to thrive after extremely aversive events? PubMed. https://pubmed.ncbi.nlm.nih.gov/14736317/

Brach, T. (2004). Radical Acceptance: Embracing Your Life With the Heart of a Buddha (Reprint ed.). Bantam.

Braden, G. (2015). Resilience from the Heart: The Power to Thrive in Life's Extremes (Revised, Updated ed.). Hay House Inc.

Brown, B. (2010). The Gifts of Imperfection: Let Go of Who You Think You're Supposed to Be and Embrace Who You Are (1st ed.). Hazelden Publishing.

Brown, B. (2012, March). Listening to shame. TED Talks. https://www.ted.com/talks/brene_brown_listening_to_shame?language=en

Brown, R. P., & Gerbarg, P. L. (2012). The Healing Power of the Breath: Simple Techniques to Reduce Stress and Anxiety, Enhance Concentration, and Balance Your Emotions (1st ed.). Shambhala.

Byrne, R. (2006). The Secret (10th Anniversary ed.). Atria Books/Beyond Words.

Canfield, J. (2019, December 2). Visualization Techniques to Manifest Desired Outcomes. Jack Canfield. https://www.jackcanfield.com/blog/visualize-and-affirm-your-desired-outcomes-a-step-by-step-guide/

Eastman, L. E. (2007). Overcoming the Super Woman Syndrome (1st ed.). Professional Woman Publishing.

Guiley, B. R. E. (2020, January 27). The Importance of Prayer and Meditation. Unity. https://www.unity.org/resources/articles/importance-prayer-and-meditation.

Harvard Health Publishing. (2010, July). Spending time outdoors is good for you, from the Letter. Harvard Health. https://www.health.harvard.edu/press_releases/spending-time-outdoors-is-good-for-you

Hawkins, M. D. P. D., & David R. Hawkins, M. D. P. D. (2013). Power vs. Force. Penguin Random House.
Hay, L. (1995). Heal Your Body. Penguin Random House.

HeartMath Institute. (n.d.). Chapter 01: Heart-Brain Communication. https://www.heartmath.org/research/science-of-the-heart/heart-brain-communication/